BEING IS GREATER THAN DOING

How to Awaken Your Passion,
Embrace Your Pain,
Own Your Power and
Establish Your Principles

RYAN LUI

Cover Design by Brian Montes

Edited by Katie Chambers

Formatted by Jen Henderson of Wild Words Formatting

STOP BEFORE YOU GO ANY FURTHER

DOWNLOAD THE *BEING IS GREATER THAN DOING* WORKBOOK

READ THIS FIRST

Just to say thanks for buying my book and to encourage you in
continuing to invest in yourself and the world, let me give you
the *Being is Greater than Doing* workbook 100% FREE!

Don't just read the book! Reflect on it!

TO DOWNLOAD GO TO:

www.beingisgreater.com/workboook

MAKE SURE YOU DON'T READ ALONE

"If you want to go fast, go alone. If you want to go far, go together."
– African Proverb

Invite a friend or two to read this with you and encourage
each other to become your best self! They can download the
first 4 chapters for free at beingisgreater.com and read
along with you. We all need someone to talk to!

Spread the message of other-centered self-development!

You're awesome.
Become even more!
Become your best!
—Ryan

DEDICATIONS

This book is written for all the dreamers, achievers, and helpers.
To those who long for a better world.
To those who believe in a better world to come.
To those who want to make a change in the world.
To those who hope for a brighter future.

You are significant.
You can make a difference.

ACKNOWLEDGMENTS

To Diana Seto, Joel Krahn, Johannes Weber, Laurence Vicencio, Matthew Chan, and Timothy Yeung, I couldn't have done this without you.

To my launch team, your support means more to me than you will ever know.

To my parents: Mom, Dad and Greg, thank you for your unconditional agape love which has shaped me more than I will ever realize.

To Vanessa, Jordan, Brenden, Diana, Bonny, Melissa, Kelly and my family, thank you for being a stable and safe place I can always come to. Filled with and full of love.

To Amanda N, Andrew Z, Benson L, Dan K, David M, Edwin C, Evelyn C, James H, Jane T, Jess W, Jon Chen, Jordan Chang, Jordan Cheng, Joshua DB, Ken P, Landon A, Lawson C, Lucas Y, Ryan P, Steph C, Steven W, and Tim I,

Thank you for allowing me to be me, for the patience, space, grace, and friendship that has allowed me to discover my identity, discern my calling, and develop into the person I am today. Thank you for your friendship. Thank you for the good news that you embody and bring to me and to all those you know.

To Tenth and my wonderful community, thank you for your partnership in figuring-out and following my calling. Thank you for your koinonia.

To every single person that has supported me in this book and in me becoming my best, thank you. I'm sorry I could not list you out by name but know that this part of the entire book was the hardest to write by far. Really. Your mentorship, partnership, and friendship has impacted me.

To those reading, I am the fruit of all these amazing people that put up with me and bless me. I am the product of a great family, great friends, and a great community. I hope everyone would be able to experience what I have been given.

With deep gratitude and joy,

Ryan

TABLE OF CONTENTS

SECTION 1

Intro

INTRODUCTION

Best Starts with Be

"At bottom every man knows well enough that he is a unique being, only once on this earth; and by no extraordinary chance will such a marvelously picturesque piece of diversity in unity as he is, ever be put together a second time."

— Friedrich Nietzsche

"When we love, we always strive to become better than we are. When we strive to become better than we are, everything around us becomes better too."

— Paulo Coelho

I don't know about you, but I've never quite perfectly fit in.

Sometimes it's strikingly obvious, and other times it's more subdued.

Whether it's conscious or not, you and I have a certain and particular understanding of how we should be. How we should live and how we should act. At some point in our childhood, we realized that we had to fit a certain mold or else.

Or else we wouldn't fit in.

Or else we wouldn't be successful.

Or else we wouldn't be happy.

Or else whatever.

At first it was just about fitting in, but as we get older, that "or else" became more and more ingrained into our minds and over time became the dominating script we lived by, leading us to either conformity or conflict. Assimilation or decimation.

But this is just the natural order of culture. Our society, and every society in history, was built upon valuing certain characteristics, people, and roles. Every society and every culture tells its people to be a certain type of person and to live a certain way.

But where has that gotten us?

Though in some ways we may have "evolved" or improved from societies in the past, can any of us say we've truly made it?

Let's just get it out there, "something" has officially hit the fan.

More accurately, "something" hit the fan a long time ago, and it's been raining down ever since. It's all over the walls, the floor, and even our faces. My apologies for the graphic depiction.

Something needs to change.

You might not be able to articulate it, but maybe you feel it.

BEING IS GREATER THAN DOING

When was the last time you thought, "Wow, isn't life great? Isn't the world just swell. I love my job. I'm so thankful I'm single. I'm so sure this person is the one I want to spend every waking moment with. Everything is happening as it should be, and nothing, not the world's, my friend's or my own life needs anything else."

Please.

We need change. Not just a change, but like real change.

We need more.

More . . .

Goodness.
Truth.
Love.
Beauty.
Safety.
Joy.
Compassion.

The list goes on.

We need more, and people are getting desperate.

Britain left the EU.
People have websites out there to help them cheat.
Men are marrying dolls and buying panties in vending machines.
Human trafficking is rampant throughout the world and our own backyard.
Racism still exists.
The cause of the #metoo movement.
The alt-right movement.

Women are still not paid equally.
And let's not get started on American politics.

Something is not quite right to say the least.

Someone call Chuck Norris, Liam Neeson, and the Avengers because, Houston, we got a problem.

A big, major, freaking problem.

As an optimist or simply a person who hasn't totally given up, I believe something can change. In fact, I need to believe something can change. Or else we're just all . . . screwed.

But what are we supposed to do? As someone who has tried doing what his parents and society told him and someone who has tried following his heart, I've learned and continue to learn that life is just way too complicated for either of those solutions. I've . . .

Listened to my parents and received a prestigious business degree.
Lived the college-boy life.
Followed my heart to become an actor.
Moved to China to volunteer with disabled orphans.
Read as many self-help books I could find.
Hosted and led personal-growth groups.
Mentored people both older and younger than me.
Brought people to self-help presentations, seminars, and courses.

I tried doing what society told me and tried following my heart. And in all my attempts to either fill that obvious void in my heart, other people, or the world, I've learned one thing:

You and I are unique.

Special.

BEING IS GREATER THAN DOING

I have and am becoming more and more convinced that you and I have been uniquely and purposefully created, wired, designed to be a certain person and to live a certain life.

No two people in the world will ever live the same life nor should they.

No two people in the world are the same. No one should ever feel they have to be anyone other than who they were born to be.

Gary Vaynerchuk is a big-time investor and advisor to Uber, Snapchat, Facebook and other major companies. He is estimated to be valued at fifty million dollars. He is an in-demand speaker to conferences and signed a ten-book deal with HarperStudio for over a million dollars. In 2014, he was named Fortune's 40 Under 40. (Thanks Wikipedia)

When pressed between choosing the importance of self-awareness vs hustling as the key to success, Vaynerchuk said without a doubt self-awareness.

Self-awareness, knowing yourself, is the ultimate determinant of your happiness, fulfillment, and "success." It is also the only thing you can actually control. You can't decide or control your own future or the futures of those around you.

All you can do is learn about yourself and make rational decisions each day according to it.

I'm not saying that what you do doesn't matter; it matters a lot. But what matters more, what matters most is who you are and who you are becoming.

You can do a lot of good stuff and for good reasons, but what I've learned is that it's ultimately going to let someone down if you're not doing it out of you, from your true and authentic self.

Being is greater than doing.

We need to stop defining success so narrowly and expand our understanding of it. A good life, a life well lived, a successful life, is one in which a person became the person they were born to be and lived out their unique calling in life.

It doesn't matter how much money you made, how many achievements you earned, or even how many people you helped, what matters most is if you became the best version of yourself. All the other stuff just said will overflow out of our best self and best life and will come naturally if it's meant to be.

Our best life is the life in which we be-came the be-st version of ourselves.

Aren't you tired of doing what the world or society tells you to do?

Aren't you tired of doing what just isn't you?

The world doesn't need more people living inauthentic lives, driven by cultural and societal pressures.

The world does need people who have a strong sense of self and who become more and more their best self. That is different for everyone. For some people it might mean they need to work less, for others to work harder. For some it might mean they need to submit to the culture, and others to reject it. For some it might mean to do what's best for their happiness, and some to do what's best for others.

The world will change when we truly value ourselves and value others.

So whether it's in the reading of books, the taking of personality tests, or even watching Netflix, I try to approach every moment and everything as an opportunity. An opportunity to learn more about myself, how I am different than others, and to come one step closer to knowing how I should truly live and who I truly am—underneath all the walls I've built, the masks I've put on, and the lies I've been told and tell.

Nobody can tell you how to live or give you your life plan. Not Donald Sutherland, Julianne Moore, or Isaiah Washington.

Certainly not I. Anyone who suggests or even thinks that they can give you your life plan, should just go back to the Hunger Games or whatever post-apocalyptic, young-adult world they came from.

Because you and I are different. Because you are unique, special, one in seven billion, no one can tell you exactly who you are or what you should do.

All anyone can do is *help* you know you: share some insights, share experiences, ask some good questions, and leave the rest to you.

And that's all this book will try to do.

I believe the best writers, the best mentors, the best people, comfort the conflicted and challenge the comfortable. And that is what I hope to do for you wherever you are on this journey we call life.

I promise that if you keep reading and give this self-awareness thing a try and really apply what you learn to your life, things are going to change. Big things. Major things.

You will:

- Have an answer to the meaning of life.

- Know yourself better than you do right now.

- Be more confident in who you are and the gift you are to the world.

- Be easier on yourself and embrace your limitations.

- Have a simple, flexible plan for personal development for the rest of your life.

- Be more effective in loving and helping those you care about.

- Stop going through the motions of life and start living your own.

I realize I'm making some big promises here. But I truly believe that everything changes when we know who we are and strive to become our best.

Don't be the person who puts off the important things in life for another day.

Be the person you were meant to be. The person your spouse/future spouse wants and needs you to be. The person your children/future children want and need you to be.

Be the kind of person other people see and say, "That person is so true to themselves. How do they do it?" Be the kind of person that prompts people to ask you, "How do you do you?"

Don't be the person who caves into society or the person who rejects society.

You don't deserve it. Your friends, family, and this world certainly don't either.

You deserve to live and be your best.

It is your right, your destiny, your calling.

BEING IS GREATER THAN DOING

"You do you" is no longer just the millennial form of encouragement. It is the prophetic call of our time to be our true and best self for the sake of the world. But for you to do you, you must be you. And for you to be you, you must know you.

If you want to live a life worth living, one with clarity and that's true to who you are,

If you want to make a difference in someone's life and the world,

Then I encourage you, I implore you, I beg you, I double-freaking dare you,

Keep reading.

Join me in the complicated but exciting journey of self-discovery, personal development, and world impact.

You, your family, your friends and our world can't afford you not to.

Be your best. Live your best. Give your best.

Because being is greater than doing.

CHAPTER 1

Who's the Boss? You're the Boss

> "You will lead this country whether you like it or not;
> you are the president of the United States."
>
> —Presidential advisor to the president
> in the television show, 24.
>
>
> "The most difficult lie I have ever contended
> with is this: life is a story about me."
>
> —Donald Miller

You are a boss.

Yes, you heard me correctly. You, are a boss.

Not a bause, but a boss.

In our fluid vocabulary, the word boss has two different connotations. One refers to someone who abuses their power. The other is a sort of compliment or term of endearment: "That's boss!"

I don't mean boss in either of those senses.

But you are the boss of your company. If we break down these terms, you will understand what I mean.

Boss

A boss in maybe its broadest sense is someone who is in a position of power and responsibility within a company. For the sake of this conversation, boss refers only to the owner of the company and not middle management.

Company

The word company comes from the Latin word "com" for "together and "panis" for "bread," which translated as one means "with bread." Thus, a company is simply a group of people working together for bread, for sustenance, for life.

The boss of such a company, then, is the one who is ultimately responsible for the profit and success of their company as well as the welfare of their customer.

Customer

A customer in the more basic of definitions is someone who has given something in return for something else. Traditionally this was conducted as barter and trade. Nowadays we use this thing called money.

As the boss of your life, you are always in trade with others whether you like it or not. Aside from maybe your mother, every other relationship you have is somehow conditional, even your spouse. At some point, if you ceased to be who you are, or treat people how you treat them, you will lose them.

We all know that good bosses care about more than just their own success and bottom-line profits. Great bosses care about their customers. They aren't thinking of how to sell them something that they don't need but rather how they can make, improve, or provide something that their customer values, which naturally results in a monetary exchange.

So knowing all this, let me repeat again: you are the boss of your own company. If the currency of life is happiness, then the customers in your life are simply the people who bring some sort of value to you, and who expect you to bring value to them.

As the boss, you have a duty and responsibility to these people. You have a responsibility to ensure that as much as they are providing value to your life, you are continually providing them with an equal if not greater amount.

In order to be the good boss of the company that is your life, you need to be concerned not just with your own happiness, but the ultimate well-being of every person who brings value to your life.

Don't be an Enron. Be an Elon Musk.

The World

Like any company however, you live within a market. You live within a community, a globalized society. There are people that you might not deal with regularly but are nonetheless somehow affected by you. This is everyone that you wouldn't consider friend or family. They are your barista, the homeless guy on the way to work, the Vietnamese lady who sewed your shirt, and the fish in the ocean.

The market is our world.

We do not live or operate in a vacuum. Though we may care most about those closest to us in our lives, our lives and choices affect more than just them.

As more and more businesses awaken to the importance of sustainability and social ethics, we must follow suit. Your happiness cannot be approached or pursued without considering the broader world.

If every company tried to give nothing to the world and get something back, then the world would go to hell. If you try to live your life taking as much as possible while giving as little as possible back, then your life is one giant Ponzi scheme and you are no better than the executives of Enron.

However, business doesn't need to be looked upon with disdain. Business is actually good and beautiful when a company, or a person, chooses to provide a quality product or service to the world.

As the boss of your life, responsible for the profit of your life and the well-being of your employees, you need a good, growing product.

As the boss of your company, you will give something to the world whether you want to or not. But you do get to choose what you will give the world and the quality of your product.

BEING IS GREATER THAN DOING

One of the most influential professors in my master's studies was a man by the name of Paul Stevens. He was my professor in the philosophy and meaning of work. In an age when everyone either wants to never work or spend all their time working, we desperately need a greater and deeper understanding of work and, ultimately, the meaning of life.

Paul said something that will always resonate with me.

We are human *beings,* not human *doings.*

However, when we think about the purpose of life, we instinctively think about it as a function or matter of doing things. We ask, "What am I supposed to do?" and "What should I be doing with my life?" And though this is certainly relevant and crucial to our lives, we are putting the cart before the horse.

One of the fundamental beliefs I have in writing to you is that you are unique. You are one of a kind. One in seven billion.

You are a person with a unique and special set of passions, life experiences, strengths, and beliefs.

You are not a cog in the wheel, a battery for the machines, or a slave to the man.

You are a boss, a free agent, an entrepreneur. You are responsible.

And if you want to provide a good product to produce as much profit, you need to know the company you run.

Each of us has built a company (life), whether intentionally or not, with a particular set of employees (people) and product (personhood).

And if every company is essentially dependent on its product, you must ask "What is my product?"

I will always remember hearing Craig Groeschel say, "When you know who you are, you know what to do."

Yes, what we do matters.

But what we do comes out of who we believe we are. None of us should be doing something in conflict with our identity. But do we really know who we are?

What you do flows out of who you are. Your behavior is the fruit of your being.

I wonder what would happen if we all thought of ourselves as human *beings* and not human *doings*. If we focused our lives on the research and development of ourselves and less on our status, success, or security.

Unfortunately, somehow we come to the conclusion that we are what we do.

We associate, if not equate, our profession to our personhood.

"Hi, I am Ryan, and I am a(n) accountant, teacher, firefighter, businessman."

You are so much more than just a job, however. Yet you have been programmed to think and live otherwise.

In order to know who you are, and, thus, what you are to do in life, you need 4 things to happen. You need to . . .

Awaken your passion.
Embrace your pain.
Own your power.
Establish your principles.

I call this the Four Pillars of Personhood. When you know who you are, when you know your passions, pains, powers, and principles, and live according to them, you live out your purpose. You offer the world the best possible product you have: your best self.

Recently, a new term has developed called "girlboss." I love that word because it shows me where the world is going.

More and more women are embracing their bosshood and living it out. Beyoncé, Brené Brown, Jessica Alba, Sarah Jessica Parker, Malala Yousafzai, and many more, married or single, old or young, are living the boss life and making a difference in the world. They're standing up against the arbitrary cultural limitations and values that have been put on them, rising above it, empowering women and men everywhere, and making the world a better place.

I heard that after Sarah Jessica Parker watched *True Cost*, a documentary on Netflix about ethical fashion and the enormous influence the fashion industry has in the world, she decided to only buy used clothing for her kids (except track pants for her boys because they tear so easily).

Malala Yousafzai, the youngest Nobel-Prize laureate in the world for her activist work in the world, wrote her autobiography: *I am Malala: The Girl Who Stood Up for Education and Was Shot by the Taliban.* It is amazing and was a pleasure to read. Just the title alone shows how much of a boss she is. Years later she is now speaking around the world, advocating for education, and making the world a better place.

DANG.

These women are living out their passions by leveraging their power in response to their pain and principles. SJP is doing what she can in the situation she is in for children everywhere in the world, probably, I can assume, out of compassion for children derived from having her own.

Malala's passion for education and her pain from being deprived of it has now become a voice for girls' education everywhere.

If the profit of your life is happiness, and the product that you offer the world is your self, then in order to ensure a thriving and growing profit, you need to do some major investment in research and development.

You need to know who you are, grow, flourish, and become your best possible self.

When you continue to grow and thrive as a person,

your product gets better and your customers are happier
your management gets better and your employees are happier
your profits get better, and you get happier.

When you become a better person—your best possible self—everyone wins. You win. Your friends win. Your family wins. The world wins.

Marianne Williamson said, "The purpose of our lives is to give birth to the best that is in us. It is only through our own personal awakening that the world can be awakened. We cannot give what we do not have."

You are a boss, and you will provide a product to the world whether you choose to do so or not. The question is, will you provide the highest quality product possible? Will you provide and thus be your best you?

In the next four chapters, I will go into detail about what exactly I mean by passion, pain, power, and principles and how to find your own. In the following chapters after that, I will provide the Six Practices to Personhood that you can live by that will support you for the rest of your life in finding your true self and being your best.

SECTION 2

The Four Pillars of Personhood

CHAPTER 2

Awaken Your Passion: You Are What You Love

Part 1: Know Who You Love and What You Love

> "The human problem is not that our passions and desires are too strong, but that they are too weak."
>
> —Greg Ogden

> "Our wants and longings and desires are at the core of our identity, the wellspring from which our actions and behavior flow."
>
> —James K.A. Smith

What are you passionate about? That's a question that's certainly popular. Whether it's at a job interview, a date, or at the coffee shop when you're trying to work, people just love to ask this question.

Passion. It's something we all know exists, but if you've ever been on either end of the question, you'll know that it's a pretty hard question to answer (especially when people expect a one-word answer). In icebreakers I've been in, and I've been in my fair share of icebreakers, maybe the only thing worse than being asked to describe myself with the first letter of my initials (I'm radical Ryan because I'm . . . radical?) is being asked to tell a stranger my passion point blank in 30 seconds.

"Hi, I'm Ryan, and I . . . have a passion for fashion?"

I honestly don't know what else I'm supposed to say. It's not that I lack passion; it's just kind of weird to talk about something so personal and intimate. It's also hard to help my listener understand why I am passionate about whatever I said in such a brief conversation.

Passion is this intense, indescribable feeling that makes us do crazy and unimaginable things. It could cause you to quit your job and leave the comfort of your life for the one you've always wanted. It could also cause momentary change like when you lose all reason and inhibitions and go home with someone you know you shouldn't, and in retrospect, still know you shouldn't have, but did anyway.

How can passion mean so many different things?

Whenever we think about words, I think it's always helpful to think about the origin of the word and its original meaning.

Passion historically has meant suffering. It comes from the Latin word "passio" meaning "suffering." (Fun fact, we learned "com" in company means "with" and so "compassion" means "to suffer with.")

So what is passion? Is it a feeling? Yea, for sure. Is it suffering? Yes, it is that too. Maybe in its most general sense then passion is having strong enough affections to make you willing to suffer for it.

BEING IS GREATER THAN DOING

Do I like fashion? Oh yes, you better believe it.

Am I willing to quit my job and suffer for an internship with Meryl Streep or line up in the sketchy area of Chinatown for those overpriced sneakers? No way, Jose.

Would I say I have a passion for fashion then? Probably not.

I think the best things in life always come from passion: out of an intense love and the suffering that comes with it. Like babies. Like you and I.

Babies are amazing. They were formed by one of the most intimate and intense acts we can perform as humans. Then the mother has to carry around this growing bowling ball in her belly as she pukes and gains weight. Then she has to push it out of herself for hours on end, leaving her body never fully the same. If babies were not made this way, I wonder if we would appreciate them the same.

Would our dream job then really be that great if we didn't have to suffer, risk, or sacrifice anything for it? Would our ideal life partner be that great if we didn't have to wait and go through the god-awful process of dating?

Love and suffering makes things valuable. No love, no suffering, no value.

Passion makes life valuable. I'd find it very hard to be convinced that a life without love, or with little love, or without suffering would make for any sort of great life. It would make for an easy life, but not one I'm sure is worth living.

If you remember grade 8 English, the components of a story are setting, character, conflict, climax, and resolution. And a good story is always one with a lot of conflict over something important. Donald Miller frames it best in that a story could involve a person working really hard, hustling, and risking her life, but if that girl turns out to be saving up to buy a Volvo instead of supporting her child or pursuing her dream, we are not going to like that story.

Great conflict for a great cause makes for a great story.

This explains why they can make three Taken movies and a TV show and why there can be so much pain and death in *Game of Thrones*, *The Walking Dead*, and *Breaking Bad*, and yet we'll keep watching.

Actively suffering for who and what we love is what makes a good story, and I would argue, a good life.

Passion is important. It's not just something we watch on TV or that the lucky few find. It's something we need for our own well-being and the well-being of others. If no one suffered for someone or something they love, I feel like we'd be in a boring and meaningless world.

Awakening to your passions, knowing who and what you love, and who and what you are willing to suffer for then is essential in becoming your best and living your best life yet.

Love: Who and What do You Love?

But how do you pinpoint, purpose, and ultimately persist in your passion?

Passion, as I have suggested, is the function of an intense feeling of love and suffering.

"Why hasn't she texted me back yet?"
"Maybe the text didn't go through."
"Maybe she missed it."
"Maybe I should text her again."
Three text messages and a sad-face selfie later . . .

No one knows love and suffering until they find themselves in the "Should I text them again?" mindset.

But is that all that passion is? Being on the verge of delusional, obsessive, and painful infatuation?

Because of our culture and its obsession with romance, we instinctively relate and even equate love to the romantic. This, however, was not always the case.

Relational Loves

Going back to thinking of words, it is always a good idea to look to the Greeks. Greek culture and language has affected our world more than we could ever imagine. They influenced Roman culture, which influenced the Mediterranean, which influenced Europe, which influenced us North Americans. The Greco-Roman world produced some of the greatest art, philosophers, thoughts, and architecture our world has ever known. They also did a lot of messed up stuff too, but that's not super relevant for our discussion.

In ancient Greek, there were six words in total all used to articulate the word that we use and know of as "love." I'm going to talk about four of them.

Eros-Being in love (the love of romantic lovers). This is the love that most of us are familiar with. The butterflies. The euphoria. It's when you got chills, and they're multiplying.

Storge-Affection (the love of a parent). This is the love that a parent has for their child where they will do anything for them and will kill a bear with their bare hands if they have to.

Philia-(the love of friends). Though we don't normally associate love with friendship, certainly there are friendships that go deeper and beyond two friends enjoying each other's company. This is the feeling of reconciling with a good friend after a fight or reuniting with an old friend after a long time.

Agape-(the unconditional love of charity). This is the love that we may feel towards a person or group of people we have no reason or condition to love. It's the feeling you get when you see those poor but happy kids on TV and just want to hug them and tell them how wonderful they are.

As someone who has been in a relationship, romantic or otherwise, you know there is something more than a simple appreciation for the other person or party. You might not describe it as *love*, but there is something more than just a feeling. And for anyone who has been in any of these relationships long enough, you will also know there is suffering. There is suffering in the romance, but there is also suffering in the parenting, the advocating of the voiceless, and the friendship.

Life is neither perfect nor easy and once you spend enough time with someone, you're bound to suffer, they're bound to suffer, and you both are bound to suffer with each other or because of each other.

These are what I refer to as the relational loves. The kinds of love that are related to people and in the context of a relationship.

Eternal Loves

Then there are what I call the eternal or virtuous loves. A love that is greater and bigger than any one person. Plato called these the three great virtues, and they have been used and reflected upon for the last twenty centuries, affecting religion and philosophy. These three virtues are:

BEING IS GREATER THAN DOING

The true.

The good.

The beautiful.

Simple words, but sometimes the simplest of things can also be the most profound. Although we use these words every day to describe different things, do we truly know what we are saying?

What exactly is true in the world? Is there anything we can say that is ultimately and objectively true?

What is good? How do we know what the difference is between right and wrong beyond our own opinions and feelings?

What is beautiful? Is beauty real or is it the subjective opinion of a culture? Is it fair to say certain things are beautiful and others are not?

In order to know your purpose in life, you need to know who you are. And the people and virtues that you love are part of what makes you who you are.

We, obviously, all love a different set of people all to different degrees. For those with children, you will have this love for them that will probably precede every other love you possess. If you are single, however, it is harder to determine whom you love and how you should live. Does your purpose in life involve your parents more or your potential future children? Do I save for my potentially non-existent future children's university tuition or shower the girl I'm seeing with flowers and trips to Europe?

We also value and love truth, goodness, and beauty differently. Your truth is most likely different than my truth. What you think is good will most likely be different than what I think is good. And almost certainly we will both disagree on what is beautiful aside from a pair of knee-high Christian Louboutin's. And so in order to know your purpose and who you are, you need to know what you believe to be good, true, and beautiful, and then what you really love out of them.

We are limited and finite beings who simply don't have the capacity to feel about and actively love all things in the world equally. I may love history and science, both provide truth and a greater appreciation for the universe. However, I just don't have the time to learn and pursue the truth and beauty of both, so I need to know which I love more.

Summary

- Passion is love and suffering.

- We have two types of love in the world. The relational: love for spouse, child, friend and charity. The eternal: the true, good, and beautiful.

- You must know who and what you love in the world and to what extent in order to know what to do in life.

Part 2: How Will You Love and What Is at Stake?

"Love and work are the cornerstones of our humanness."

—Sigmund Freud

"The starting point of all achievement is desire. Keep this constantly in mind. Weak desires bring weak results, just as a small amount of fire makes a small amount of heat."

—Napoleon Hill

If figuring out your purpose was as easy and simple as figuring out who or what you love, you would probably be happier and more focused in life. The world would be a better place by now.

As much as "find your passion" or "love what you do and do what you love" are great motivational slogans and looks great on a mug, are they all that helpful?

When it comes to passion, you need to not just ask *what* you love but also *how* you love? How do you most naturally express your love for others and for truth, goodness, and beauty?

More often than not, we are told there is only one way to pursue our passion. That there is only one way to love. But if we looked even briefly at the diversity of people, we would quickly discover that there is never one exact way to love somebody or something. We are all different and unique and have our own personal preferences and expressions of love.

Although passion starts with love, it is expressed in labor.

Labor-How do you love?

Gary Chapman-The 5 love languages

In relationships, there are five ways people express their love according to Dr. Gary Chapman, author of the widely popular book *The 5 Love Languages: The Secret to Love that Lasts*. According to Chapman, we express and receive our love differently:

1. Receiving and giving gifts

2. Serving or receiving an act of service

3. Quality time

4. Words of affirmation

5. Physical touch

For me, I'm definitely words of affirmation, then quality time, then physical touch.

When someone affirms my qualities that I feel unsure about, I feel very loved and appreciated.

For quality time, I don't need to do anything exciting or big; I just need to know that my presence is appreciated. That when I'm with someone, romantically or not, I know they wouldn't want to be anywhere else in that moment.

I also appreciate hugs despite my Asian reservedness and time with people. Side hugs, front hugs, back hugs, show me you appreciate me! (To all those inclined to think physical must mean sexual, it does not!)

Gifts and service are at the bottom for me. It's why I loathe and dread Christmas and birthdays. I can't stand the pressure of having to think about a gift to buy for someone. I don't even like receiving them (I have specific tastes). I'm the kind of guy that just wants to share a meal and some stories, play some board games, and maybe watch a movie.

If you grew up in any way like I did, you grew up with people around you that loved you. You probably, however, also grew up frustrated and never feeling fully loved. To no one's fault other than the complexity and finiteness of the human person, you didn't receive exactly what you needed in every moment of your life.

That's life for you, though.

If you love someone, then you will want to love them well. Not everything can be resolved and not everyone will be blessed with money or a gift. In order to properly pursue your passion for the people in your life well, you must know how you express love as well as how they receive it.

Tom Rath-StrengthsFinders 2.0

I'll go into this in a bit more depth later on in chapter 4, but to make it brief, Don Clifton, Gallup Inc., along with Tom Rath, created an assessment and profile made up of 34 strengths. Each of us naturally possess particular talents or potential that can become strengths in greater qualities than others. None of us are perfect, right? And within these 34 strengths, they can be categorized into four types: execution, influence, relationship building, and strategic thinking. In my own words:

Doing
Motivating
Connecting
Thinking

Though they are usually presented as strengths or talents, they are also representative of our natural and joyful ways of expressing our relational and eternal love.

Have you ever just wanted to be heard, listened to, or joined in spirit as you shared the hardships and heartaches of life? But instead, the person you are speaking to without solicitation offers you a five-step plan on how to get out of it, a list of reasons why it's your fault you're in this mess, or just tells you that what you're feeling or doing is dumb and irrational.

I know I have (been on both ends).

And whenever my friend, Dad, or random acquaintance would do this, I have to hold all that is within me while smiling and resisting the urge to just go off.

"Like did I ask for your unsolicited advice?"

Something I've learned over the years is that we express our love in different ways. Unfortunately, the reality is that they are not always the best, wisest, or most tactful of ways. Though your loved ones do love you (maybe not the random acquaintances) and they are trying their best to help you, their help is based on what they know about helping people (which is usually very little), how they have been taught, and how they naturally express their love.

Sure, there's a place for a five-step plan, an honest conversation about the consequences of your decisions, and how you need to just wake up and not be an idiot. Yes, this is certainly needed a lot in our lives, but it's just usually needed and appreciated (hopefully) later when we've thought things out and processed our feelings.

My friend, Jane, has the "Command" strength. Basically it's what you think it is: she's bossy. She doesn't have much tact and often causes the people around her to feel frustrated, unless they're fairly emotionally healthy or want that type of hard love. But Jane's great at organizing events and getting stuff done. Though she has no formal credentials, she's the type of person you'd ask to organize your wedding. The friend you can always count on to get stuff done and the one you always put in charge. This is what she's good at, and this is also, we could say, how she expresses her passion.

Jane likes to boss people around, to tell people what to do. Now although we may consider this primarily a negative and unnecessary skill in the complex world of emotions and language, Jane's preference to command is, at the end of the day, necessary. From generals to managers, we need people who can just cut the crap, say it how it is, and get things done. If everyone approached every hard conversation as a kindergarten teacher, nothing that needs to get done now would ever get done. Sure, a lot less feelings would be hurt, but would anything get done?

Whenever I would tell her about a problem with my dad, my friends, or dating, she would always tell me to take this course. It seemed like every conversation we had would inevitably end in "You should go take this course." Most people would tune her out; most people in fact do. But because I knew she truly cared for me and loved me, I tried my best to take her words for what they were.

Eventually she "convinced" me to take the course. In this year-long course (ten months of weekly 2.5 hour meetings where I'd sit with a group of five other men and talk about our relational problems with women, men, parents, and everyone in between), I experienced one of the most formative and amazing journeys of my life. I'm indebted to the course, and I'm certainly indebted to Jane.

I'm grateful she told me exactly what I needed to hear and do.

My friend, Jane, is well aware of her strength as the commandeering and type-A, bossy pants. And as someone whom I greatly respect because of her capacity for emotional maturity and thoughtfulness, she is continually thinking her conversations through, sometimes saying the wrong things, and often times, if not all times, thinking back and either apologizing or learning from the experience.

Jane, however, along with all the people in our lives who are gifted with "get crap done" talents and strengths will always suffer (and make us suffer) as they learn to live out their natural expressions of love. But it is not just those like Jane whose love will include suffering. The kindergarten teachers in our lives will suffer and cause us to ultimately suffer too when they don't speak the truth, avoid it, or sugar coat it all the time.

Passion is love and labor. We suffer in our love when it is not reciprocated. But there is also suffering in the labor. There's work. It is work. Love is a verb, and when we "do love," sometimes it's appreciated and received, and often times it's not. In order to live out your purpose, you are going to have to identify your passion. You must know whom you love, what you love, and also how you naturally love.

BEING IS GREATER THAN DOING

Autonomy, Mastery, and Purpose

Daniel Pink's book, *Drive,* is a classic in human resource management, leadership, sociology, psychology, and general human understanding. It's a good book to say the least. Without even knowing it, I have read three of his books, and he is actually one of the only writers whom I have read and own more than two of his writings.

In *Drive,* Pink suggests that due to the rapid and vast development of our society, we seek different things than before. We want the "higher" stuff of life. We, for the most part, have our physical and relational needs met. What we want then is a way of living marked by personal fulfillment.

This is not to say that this desire is not universal, but because of the pressures and realities of the world, often those older and in different parts of the world were not or have not been gifted with the opportunities that most of us enjoy and, therefore, are not as concerned with concepts such as meaning or purpose.

So why is Pink so awesome for me? Well, because I believe he has simply captured the essence of what we all want in our work.

We want to be autonomous. We don't want to be told what or how to do things, and we certainly don't want to be micro managed.

We want to be masters. Gone are the days when we could just clock in, do the bare minimum, and go home happy. We want to continually grow and become our absolute best at our work.

We also want our work to be part of a greater purpose. We want to know that our work is somehow bringing truth, goodness, and beauty into the world.

We want a vocation, not a profession. We want a calling and not just a career.

Although Pink wrote this primarily in regards to our desires for work, I believe that this extends far beyond what we do for a living and expresses the core of human flourishing.

I don't want to be told how to do my job; I also don't want to be told how to live my life. I don't want to simply be good at doing things; I want to be a good person. I want to continually become better and ultimately my best. And I don't just want my work to have meaning; I want everything I do and every moment of my life to also.

If life is ultimately about love—receiving it, yes but primarily giving—then how we want our work life to be like is in many ways how we want our life (of love) to be as well.

We love best when we have autonomy, mastery and purpose. In considering these principles, we realize we want to love others and the world the way we want to, the way that makes us a better person, and for a greater purpose.

If we want to pursue our passion and ultimately love well, we need to be aware of what we need in order to do so.

Is an easy-going person who will appreciate whatever expression of love you give, no matter how grand or lame, important for you?

Or do you need someone who loves you for a greater purpose rather than just their own happiness?

You want to create goodness, truth, and beauty in this world, but you are realizing that the way the world has told you how doesn't work for you. You want to do it your own way with all your heart and soul.

You want to do it in your work, but you also want to do it in your life. You have a side hustle. You're taking an online course. You started a blog.

How we love others and the world is simply no longer the single acts we perform but rather a way of being. A way of life. To know how you are to love is then to know how you should live.

Pink's research and work may not be the most practical, but it is necessary as it encourages and affirms that desire in your heart for more.

You have been created uniquely, wired specifically, and that is very good.

Legacy-What is at stake?

As someone who practically lives in the future, I wonder right now as I write these words who might be reading this in months and years to come. What good, if any, will it do? What good will I have done?

There is a part of me that hopes that everyone, including you, after reading this, in a rush of excitement and motivation, would begin voraciously reading much better and much more helpful books to help you discover yourself and plan your life. I hope you will pursue meaningful conversations with others who have thought about and pursued the meaning of life. And I hope that, ultimately you will be one step, if not miles, closer to living your best.

When we think about our passions, we don't just ask what/whom we love and how we will work/suffer to love them, but also,

Who and what is at stake?

I believe the final piece that we often miss when thinking about purpose and passion is the *long run.*

I am writing this book because I believe that something needs to fundamentally change.

I believe that we want to and have to be better. We have to be our best possible selves for the sake of our souls and the sake of those we love. If you are not able to take responsibility and ownership of the company which is your life, you will not be able to flourish as the person you were made to be.

I wrote this book, however, not just because you and the world are at stake, but because my own life and personal world is at stake too.

I have known for quite a while that I love to write. I'm a communicator at heart. And what I have realized as I have written this book is that if I don't write, I deny my passion. And to deny my passion is to deny part of who I am.

As someone who truly believes that we must, for the sake of our souls and the world, live and be our best, how can I not then model this life as much as I can? If I don't pursue my passions in this life, why would anyone? And if I do not pursue my passions, and you don't either, then is the world or anything ever going to change?

So who and what is at stake for you? Why must you love this person, these people, or this virtue? What would or would not happen if you didn't?

You have something in you. A desire, a passion, a love that you cannot fully explain or articulate. All you know is that if you do not do this, a part of you will die. It may be singing, it may be caring for your children, or baking pies. Whatever it is, however, you must do it. You must pursue it. For you, your friends, your family, and the world.

Summary

- How we naturally love is as diverse as who and what we love.

- We express our love through gifts, service, time, words, and touch.

- We express our love through doing, motivating, connecting, and thinking

- We express our love best when we have autonomy, mastery, and purpose

- If you do not pursue your passion, you deny yourself and the world something.

CHAPTER 3

Embrace Your Pain:
You Are Not What You Think

Part 1: Bad Backs and Bad Beliefs

> "For most people it's not what they are that holds
> them back. It's what they think they're not."
>
> —John Maxwell
>
>
> "Almost all our desires, when examined,
> contain something too shameful to reveal."
>
> —Victor Hugo

We like to talk a lot about love. Almost everything seems to be about it, whether it's in the romantic sense of relationships or the self-help sense of self-love. We think that the answer to everything is love. As the Beatles' song goes "all you need is love."

We are simply obsessed with love.

Don't get me wrong: I'm a big proponent of it—romantic love, family love, friendship love, self-love—but I'm just not quite convinced that's all we need.

Growing up, I knew my dad always loved me. Often, he would actually say it out loud and tell me, which is quite uncharacteristic for an Asian male. Well, really any Asian and any male. However, it seemed like my dad was always in a genuine state of surprise whenever he found out about anything I had accomplished or was proud of.

Have you ever done something good and someone reacted with genuine surprise?

It's kind of a double-edged sword or a back handed compliment. In one sense, the person is amazed by what you did. In another sense, they had no idea you were capable of such an accomplishment.

Because my father always reacted that way, over time my subconscious formed a belief unknown to my father or myself.

I believed that no one believed in me. That I would never accomplish anything in life. And that at the end of the day, I was expendable.

Did my Dad actually think that? No, of course not.

Did I? Yes, how could I not?

I can tell you that I never for a moment doubted that my dad loved me. I just never thought he *believed* in me. And I think there's a big difference between love and belief. We can love a lot of people, but not necessarily believe in them.

You can be told your entire life that you are loved, and that all your parents or anyone wants is for you to be happy. But it is not the same as your parents in the bleachers with face paint on, cheering you on and getting in protective fights with other parents. Other than the sports arena, very few of us ever find ourselves in situations that would permit such an affirming act of belief.

But this extends to more than just believing someone can do something. I have a lot of friends whose parents expect that they can and should be doctors, lawyers, and highly educated and successful people. But that is not the same belief I'm referring to. Just as love is not the same as beliefs, expectations are not either.

I write this book because we have a deep need to be believed in.

A need for someone to call us upward and forward.

A need for someone to say, "Hey, I believe in you."

I can only write this, however, because I have learned to embrace my pain. I have learned to accept the fact that I am human, and I unashamedly have needs. Particularly, to be believed in.

I had to acknowledge and address this gap that I had, still have, and always will have in myself. And then I had to stop trying to get my father to believe in me and turn to healthier sources of affirmation.

You need to talk about the people who have hurt you and the times which you have felt pain. You need to think critically about the lies you have been hearing, listening to, and believing all your life. And you need to honestly confess the ways in which you have been living according to them.

You need to remember and enter such painful moments that you might prefer to forget because they, whether you like it or not, are a part of your story.

Without recognizing and embracing your pain, you will never be able to become fully whole.

There are generally two different types of pain: the physical and the emotional. We all understand the physical. You cut yourself, it hurts. You touch something hot, it hurts. When things hurt, it means you shouldn't do it.

But then there is the other type of pain, the emotional pain, the pain of the heart.

Something much harder to identify and treat.

We say sticks and stones may break our bones, but words can never hurt us. But don't they hurt? In fact, a lot?

What happens when we get hurt physically? We ice it, heat it, put a Band-Aid on it, and possibly even go to the hospital. To everyone, there is a rational medical procedure and solution. Not so with our hearts.

Our hearts are a fickle thing. They are the source of our joy, hope, and excitement, and yet also of our anger, fear, and sadness.

Feeling loved and safe, which doesn't happen when people hurt our hearts, is a required need just as much as needing to physically remain safe from harm.

Abraham Maslow was a psychologist in the early nineteen hundreds who came up with this idea that there are fundamental needs all humans have and which come in a particular order or hierarchy. This later became known as Maslow's Hierarchy of Needs.

BEING IS GREATER THAN DOING

Basically, Maslow said that we have five needs: physiological, safety, love, esteem, and self-actualization. Basically, we first need things like food, shelter, and sleep. That is our physiological need. Then after we achieve those very basic things, we require a level of safety. We need to know that the world, our government, our neighbor, and strangers are not out to get us, rob us, or use us.

And then afterwards we need love, we need friendship, community. After that Maslow argues that we then need self-esteem, confidence, and respect. Respect for self as well as the respect from and for others. And then after that, self-actualization where we desire things such as purpose, creativity, and morality. But we don't start seriously thinking about or desiring these things until all the other needs below are met.

Although this model is not perfect, it is helpful in understanding the needs you and I have.

You have needs, both physical and emotional. And that's okay. In fact it's normal, human, and rightly so. You are not perfect, nor can you ever be.

In an age of haters, critics, and people who just don't understand, we are often portrayed as lazy and selfish, out of touch with the real world. We talk about and complain about trivial things, which have been part of the fabric of "adult life" since the industrial revolution. In fact, we have it good, better than anyone has ever had before.

Behind this criticism is the insinuation that our problems are not real problems. Though I agree with our critics that yes, our problems are nowhere near the catastrophes, crises, and calamities of the world ranging from poverty to human trafficking, our problems are not irrelevant or unreal either.

Our pain is our pain, and that makes it real.

All our needs are natural and good. However, like any need or desire they can be twisted. Our desire for love can be and become an emotionally unhealthy quest to be completed by another person. Our search for respect can easily become a conquest for power and control. And our search for morality, purpose, and even creativity can become a throne in which we look at the faults and brokenness of others with shame and judgment.

But as long as our needs do not become twisted, they are genuine needs and shouldn't be discounted, as we need them in order to grow and thrive. And when we are deprived of these necessary elements, we are choked of the life we crave and we learn to adapt.

We learn to find alternatives, tofu-substitutes to the needs of our soul and the desires of our heart. And who wants to ever have a tofu-substitute?

Bad Backs and Bad Beliefs

How many of you suffer from some sort of back or hip pain? I know I have and do. But because we are highly adaptive and creative creatures, if one muscle in my body is weak, or a ligament is tight, my body will find some way to keep going.

My pain wasn't from any single injury or movement that I made but rather the result of bad posture over a long time. Weak glutes, a weak core, and a pelvic tilt makes Ryan in lots of pain. Apparently, if you stand, sit, and lift weights with bad form for too long, it's going to catch up to you eventually.

Thus, the body is amazing, but it's not perfect. It can adapt and compensate for weaker areas in the body, but it can also prevent us from full mobility.

The same holds for our heart.

All of us have a bad heart posture. We live our lives and go through our days functioning but with limited flexibility.

Though there may be moments in our lives where the pain is excruciating and immobilizing, we find ways to address the pain but not the posture that follows.

For our backs we may apply an ice pack, hot gel, or see a professional. However, the pain eventually comes back if we are not persistent in our training and rehabilitation. Likewise, for our hearts, we may have a conversation or read a book that will bring us to a level of clarity and healing, but if we are not persistent in it, we will eventually find ourselves in the same pain.

Today many people are speaking of the tremendously negative impact sitting has for us. As hunter/gathering beings, we were never designed to sit on a chair and in front of a computer for eight hours a day only to come home and sit on another chair in front of our television. Dr. Kelly Starrett, author of *Becoming a Supple Leopard,* in his book *Deskbound: Standing Up to a Sitting World* argues that sitting is literally killing us.

Just as there is a routine that has led to the poor posture of our backs, so too is there one for our hearts. This routine is the continual listening to three improper beliefs about ourselves. The beliefs that we are not acceptable, capable, or loveable.

Unacceptable

The first improper belief of the heart is the one that says you are unacceptable. You aren't good enough. Not smart enough, funny enough, attractive enough, _____ enough.

We have all lived this bad belief out someway in our lives.

It doesn't matter your IQ, your culture, or upbringing, you will have times when you don't feel accepted without any reason other than because you are a human being. Who among us has ever felt 100% accepted all the time?

To feel unacceptable is ultimately to feel shame. It is the belief that "I am not good" for no other reason than that "it is true." This is not to be confused with guilt, however. Guilt despite its lack of popularity is good. Guilt says, "I made a mistake." But shame says, "I am a mistake."

The problem with this bad belief is that it is a distortion of the truth. You aren't perfect, and yes, you could use some improvement, but you are acceptable.

You were created the way you are for a reason and a purpose. You are unique. We are all different. And that is beautiful.

Shame dresses itself up as a "healthy humility" or a healthy dose of "reality." However you slice it, it's dressed up as healthy. It's good to think lowly of yourself. It's good to regularly put yourself down or look at yourself "soberly." Because only then can you see your weaknesses and do something about them.

The term weakness is misleading, unhelpful, and ultimately self-defeating, however. Gordon Smith makes a point when talking about imperfections to refer to them as limitations rather than weaknesses. When we think of a physical weakness, we instinctively in the same breath know that it should be fixed. But with a physical limitation, we understand that it is a sad reality of life that we should not dwell on any longer than we need to.

Therefore, when you talk about your imperfections, you must be careful to not confuse your limitations with weaknesses.

Shame turns your limitations into weaknesses where everything becomes an area of improvement.

It points to the filtered people on Instagram, the smiling personas on YouTube, and that one kid from high school who made it to Silicon Valley, and says, "Why aren't you like them? You should be them."

Incapable

The second improper belief we all hold is the one that we are incapable.

Western culture is arguably founded upon the values of achievement and performance. The America we know today was birthed from exuberant explorers, businessmen, and everyday men and women looking for a better life.

Whether one can "perform" is a defining factor to a person's worth. There are no participation marks or awards in life. There are only "winners" and "losers" as we are often reminded.

We live in a society of human "doings" and not human "beings."

However, while we instinctively know that the value of a child is not based upon their performance or achievement, somehow as we get older, we began valuing people and ourselves based on what we do and have done.

We bought into the lie that we are what we do.

And what's worse, that we can't do anything.

We bought into the lie that we are defined by what we have accomplished, but also that we will never accomplish anything worth celebrating.

To be called a loser, a failure, or useless is one of the easiest ways to put someone down. It's so easy because like any good lie, it is a distortion of the truth. We all want to do good and great things in this world, and yet have not done all that we wanted to or believe we can do.

Unlovable

Then there's the last improper belief: that we are unlovable.

This may be the most insidious and pervasive of all the lies.

"If they only knew who I really was."
"If they only knew what I really am."
"They wouldn't want me."
"They wouldn't associate with me."

The lie that we are unlovable tells us that we cannot be loved by a person unless we are someone other than who we are.

As we have learned, passion is a function of love and labor. To be worthy of love is to be worthy of labor. To believe that you are unlovable is then to believe that you are of no value. That you are not worth working for, fighting for, or pursuing.

If the bad belief that we are unacceptable is I am not _____ enough, the bad belief that we are unlovable says that we will never be _____. The former is about adequacy; the latter is about essence. One is about what we lack; the other is about who we are.

If I am not enough of something, there is a way to fix it if not address it. To not be something, however, is hopeless. There's absolutely nothing I can do. "I will always be _____." And it is why this may be the worst of all lies.

The lie that one is unlovable tells the person that no matter what they do, no matter what they change, no one will truly appreciate them for who they are. There will always be conditions.

Your pain, however, doesn't have to remain as it is. You do not have to live with the pain that results from your poor posture.

However, do not confuse imperfection with pain.

We all have limitations in what we can do, and that is okay. You don't need to be able to do everything. However, you also have pain. Wounds of the heart that can and should be healed. How much money do we spend on school, gym memberships, and supplements for better and stronger minds and bodies? Why then do so few of us spend the same amount of effort on our hearts?

Wouldn't you agree that a healthy heart would lead to a much greater life than a more knowledgeable mind or stronger body?

So how do we treat and heal our hearts?

The first step you must do is diagnose any and every pain that may slow you down or impede you from reaching your goal. If you had a sprained ankle or a damaged ACL, you would not keep running nor would you stop running for the rest of your life. Instead, you would see the doctor, the physio, the chiro (if you trust them), any and everybody who might be able to bring you another step closer to healing.

This is what you must do with your body, and your heart. Identify and diagnose the pain that prevents you from wholeness and begin treatment and rehabilitation. Don't give up on your goal; don't sit out. You are in the marathon of your life and the goal has been set: your best self.

You are the CEO of your life. You must identify the inefficiencies and redundancies and proceed to fix them as you continue to operate.

Summary

- Our childhoods and upbringings have all created deficits in our lives.

- These deficits have created real needs in our lives that cannot be ignored.

- We naturally attempt to fill these needs with various remedies and treatments.

- We all live whether consciously or not with three bad beliefs or lies: that we are unacceptable, incapable, and unlovable.

- In order to be healed, we need to acknowledge the pain.

Part 2: Healing and Wholeness

"If you do not transform your pain, you will always transmit it."

—Friar Richard Rohr

"We are half-hearted creatures, fooling about with drink and sex and ambition when infinite joy is offered to us, like an ignorant child who wants to go on making mud pies in a slum because he cannot imagine what is meant by an offer of a holiday at sea. We are far too easily pleased."

—C.S. Lewis

During a family vacation when I was 13, I pulled my groin. This is not to be confused with any sexual organ. One day we went tubing, and as I was hanging on for dear life on the tube, the speed and the force of the waves caused my right leg to fly off the tube and hang too far in the water, resulting in an overstretched and pulled groin.

I could barely walk or even sit the next day.

Since we were on vacation, we didn't know a nearby doctor and I didn't want to ruin the trip anyway. So what did I do? What any sensible man would do: Self-diagnose and self-treat.

What do you do when something's tight? Stretch it and work it, obviously. So all day I stretched my hip area, and when we got back to our motel, I thought swimming would be another great idea to speed up its recovery. Did it hurt as I swam? Yes, a bit. But hey, no pain no gain right?

Holy mother of all that is good in the world, never had I felt so much pain in my entire life in the following hours after my swim. My groin was burning, and I felt like crying. I don't know what childbirth is like, but that is what it felt like for me. Although swimming seemed like a good idea, it was the absolute worst thing I could and did do to myself.

After I got back, I went to see a doctor and was diagnosed with a pulled groin. I saw a physio and got out of gym class for six months. Before we could even begin rehabilitation, I had to use the stairs with only my good leg and rest up my pulled groin as much as possible.

Although, in that situation, I was an ignorant, young and prideful boy (like there's any other kind), I have as an adult, continued to diagnose and treat myself. However more often than not, the wounds I have treated were not physical but emotional.

Diagnosing and treating wounds of the body, as difficult as they are and as much as they need expert medical advice, are in ways much simpler than diagnosing and treating wounds of the heart. We know what a strong and unbroken bone feels like. We know what flexibility feels like. We know that pain is bad; thus, we should stop doing whatever is causing us pain.

But not so with matters of the heart. It's a lot more difficult to know when we are actually in pain. It's hard to stop stretching and swimming, even though it hurts. We somehow convince ourselves that it's good for us. Sure, stretching brings an amount of flexibility back to the wounded ligament or muscle, but if you've ever pulled anything, you'll know you first need to rest it and let the inflammation die down.

The same applies to our hearts. We have all sorts of emotional wounds, pulled hearts, and yet we're all stretching and swimming, bringing temporary relief, flexibility, and strength, but ultimately more pain and damage.

In order to begin the healing process to anything, you need to first just stop doing whatever is prolonging and perpetuating your pain. You need to stop stretching and stop swimming.

You need to recognize that some of the solutions you have been told or came up with on your own are false and stop them. Before you even get to stretches and exercises, the physio needs to first get you to stop doing the stupid stuff you came up with on your own.

You need to stop applying Windex on your cuts and bruises and throwing your back on top of a garbage can when it feels stiff.

While there are many improper treatments out there, we often turn to three in particular to try and self-heal the emotional damage caused by our three improper beliefs.

Three Improper Treatments

Status

When we feel the pain that comes from believing the lie that we are not acceptable, that we are not good enough, strong enough, _____ enough, we either fight or fly. We do whatever we can to fit into society. We dress, act, and do whatever the cool kids do. We create and exaggerate online personas, showing the world a version of ourselves that does not exist. In it we deny ourselves.

Success

When we buy into the lie that we are not capable, that what we do is never good enough, we live a life dedicated to proving it wrong. We get degrees and letters we can put after our email signature. We display trophies in our homes and find a way to mention our success in any and every conversation.

It's so easy to do because we tell ourselves we are simply "sharing" our successes, wins, and happiness with others. And sure there is a time, place, and people to do that with, but is it that necessary to talk about it all the time?

Security

And when we believe the lie that we are fundamentally unlovable, that there is no one in the entire world, not even our own family that could love and provide for us without a single condition, we accept what we think we deserve. For some of us that unconditional love, that sense of security, comes in the form of a one-night stand or entering into a relationship we don't really want.

In both the commitment of partnership and the contract of sex, we relieve our pain, and our sense of loneliness and insecurity, believing for however long, that we need not provide anything else. In a long term relationship all I have to provide is my self and my personality. In sex, all I must provide is my body. Unknowingly, however, we enter into a relationship that is still based on conditions and never truly provide the complete and unconditional love that we seek and need.

We mistake status, success, and security as the solution to our emotional pain. If insanity is repeating the same action and expecting a different result, then we have all, to a degree, become patients to the mental asylum of status, success, and security.

As I reflect on the bad beliefs that we are unacceptable, incapable, and unlovable, it cannot be any clearer to me that what is required is a fundamental reframing of our beliefs and the posture of our heart and life.

Rather than seeking society's traditional drugs of choice—status, success, and security—you must pursue and possess something else.

You must pursue a mended, whole, and full heart. You must bandage it up, give it rest, and slowly begin the rehabilitation process.

What does this mended, whole, and full heart look like? What does this heart pursue and possess opposed to society's offering of status, success and security? No, it's not the opposite. A life of insignificance, poverty, and celibacy may be helpful, but I don't believe they are the ultimate answer.

The solution is not so much to run and avoid status, success, and security, but rather ask what it is you are truly seeking at its core and find a healthy and truly human path to get there. As I look at the three improper beliefs and the three improper treatments we have all embraced, what we truly need and, therefore, must seek is identity, influence, and intimacy.

The need to know who we are and be comfortable in our own skin. The need to be significant and have an impact in the world. And the need for a relationship of vulnerability and trust.

Improper Belief	Improper Treatment	Proper Treatment
Unacceptable	Status	Identity
Incapable	Success	Influence
Unlovable	Security	Intimacy

Proper Treatment

Identity

All of us ask the million dollar question: "Who am I?" We were told who we were and who we should be, but we never had the chance to ask the question and learn how to answer it ourselves.

I just finished watching Netflix and Marvel's *Iron Fist*. It's the fourth in their "Everyday Heroes" series. A series of shows about ordinary men and women with slightly above ordinary powers. *Iron Fist* is about Danny Randy who was stranded in the Himalayan Mountains at the age of ten after his family's plane crashed. Danny was rescued by monks who took him to a city in another dimension where he then learned martial arts for 15 years and acquired the power and identity of the "Iron Fist."

Danny, at the ripe age of 25, decided to leave his post and role as Iron Fist, protector of the heavenly city of Kun Lun, and find his way back home to New York City and claim his identity as Danny Rand.

Through the 13-episode season, Danny is in continual conflict in discovering who he is, what really happened to his parents, and how he is to live in New York as billionaire tycoon, Danny Rand, and also as warrior monk, Iron Fist. How is he supposed to live when he has two seemingly opposing identities? Must he choose? Which is his true and real identity?

Every great story revolves around a character that discovers something about themselves. It's called character development. Whether it is the discovery of a force within them, the true identity of their father, or the reconnecting with a long-lost sister, somewhere at some point, the character must learn something of who they truly are. (Starwars is a great story).

Every great story involves self-discovery: the learning of one's true and ultimate identity, one apart from what they were told or given.

When you become aware of your identity and grow in your assurance of it, you begin to no longer believe the lie that you are unacceptable and you lose the need to prove yourself to the world.

Influence

Despite my young age, I often think about my own death. Maybe you do the same once in a while. How will I die? Will it be sudden or will I know when it's coming? I have hoped for a while that I would die by some congenital disease so I would know when it's coming and make some plans.

Funerals really suck because the person who everyone knew isn't even there. So I've thought, if I could know when I was going to die, I could arrange my funeral beforehand and hang out with everyone one last time before I left.

I don't think I'm alone in my desire. We all want a life that mattered. One in which, at the end, those who cared for us, loved us, and had been affected by us will gather together and celebrate the life we lived and the impact we had on them.

In our pursuit for success, we are constantly trying to silence the voice telling us we will never amount to anything. That our life will not have mattered. That we do not matter.

A life without influence is a life without impact. It literally is a life that made no difference positively or negatively in the world or in another's life.

However, that is not the life we want. No one can say they want a life that did not matter. A life without significance or influence.

Isn't it why we want to have children? To have a significant and positive influence on the life of another? Is it not why we volunteer or even seek positions of power? So that we may have some sort of influence and impact upon another?

Influence does not necessarily need to be a "leadership" term or one even reserved to alpha-males. It is reserved for all of humanity. It is the simple and basic desire that we all have: to have and live a life that somehow made a difference upon another.

When we seek and find a life true to our identity and full of meaningful influence in and upon the world, we give up the constant need to prove ourselves through achievement. What we seek is not success, though success may naturally come. What we seek is influence. A life that mattered meaningfully to someone.

Intimacy

Have you heard of the love test? It's a series of 36 questions followed by an intense four-minute eye-lock, designed by psychologist Arthur Aron in the 1990s to see if random strangers could fall in love. It was popularized, however, by Mandy Len Catron, a UBC lecturer in an article for the New York Times on her experiment of the test during a first date in the mid 2010s.

The test is structured to begin with fairly simple questions. The first one is "Who in history past or present would you want to have dinner with?" The questions, however, gradually become more intimate, unknowingly bringing the couple emotionally closer and closer.

If the couple goes through all 36 questions, they will have gone through a very intense yet natural revealing of their true self. They follow that with a four-minute gaze into one another's eyes which they cannot break.

Reportedly, after going through all the questions and the intimate eye-lock, the couple falls in love. This is reported by Aron as well as Catron who ended up in a serious relationship with the experiment's subject.

Though there is no hard evidence to suggest that love can simply be reduced to a staring contest and knowing certain things about a person, the principle that came out of the experiment seems valid. And that is that love is ultimately birthed out of intimacy.

Whether you are in a long-term relationship, been through many, or casually "seeing" other people, what you are seeking at the end of it all is intimacy. That one relationship where you can truly be yourself. The one in which you can be embraced warts and all, completely physically and emotionally naked.

We all want to go back to the garden where we could roam naked without the insecure feeling and need to cover ourselves up.

It's that feeling of vulnerability with trust. It's probably why sex is so appealing. Like yea being naked and wrestling each other is fun, but the climax is not the orgasm but rather the spiritual and emotional union in vulnerability and trust.

"He didn't laugh at my body."
"He stayed the next day."
"He will stay and raise our baby if we have one."

Whether it's the commitment of two lovers for twenty years, or the sensuous embrace of two strangers in two hours, there is a certain level of vulnerability and trust that is always exchanged.

Though the most traditional and arguably accessible means to such vulnerability is a romantic partner, it is not the only way.

The sharing of one's heart and soul is not confined or limited to the sharing of bodies. Can any of us confidently say that a person who has been forever single never can or will experience a friendship where vulnerability and trust meet?

I don't believe so.

We are all human and seek a relationship out there where we can be truly loved for who we are. Where we can live emotionally naked, without fear and in confidence and trust.

When you can begin to recognize the wounds of your heart, how you have mistreated yourself, and the true needs of your heart, you can begin the journey towards wholeness. You can stop harmful and self-destructive behaviors and begin forming healthy and healing habits.

And as you slowly walk and begin picking up the pace down the sunlit trail of life, you are given the sight and strength to see others on the sidelines deep in the muddy ditch, just as you once were. You can call out to them and extend a hand out of the pain and back onto the path to their whole and best self.

The beauty of life and its interconnectedness is that when we begin to discover one thing, we often find another. When we begin to identify and embrace our pain, we not only begin to heal, but we are gifted with the insight, passion, and ability to turn it into our power.

As I heard a wise woman once say, "Often those who have been hurt the most often have the greatest ability to heal." (Taken from a conversation between Michelle Yeoh from *Crouching Tiger Hidden Dragon* with Jessica Alba, talking about Jason Statham in *The Mechanic 2*.)

Summary

- There are three great lies that we can believe: we are unacceptable, incapable, and unlovable.

- We attempt to fill this need by acquiring status, success or security.

- The way to healing is moving toward identity, influence and intimacy.

CHAPTER 4

Own Your Power:
You Are What You Can

Part 1: Make It, Take It, or Break It

"You are not here merely to make a living. You are here in order
to enable the world to live more amply, with greater vision, with a
finer spirit of hope and achievement. You are here to enrich the
world, and to impoverish yourself if you forget the errand."

—Woodrow Wilson

"My life shall touch a dozen lives before this day is done,
Leave countless marks for good or ill ere sets the evening sun,
This is the wish I always wish, the prayer I always pray;
Lord, may my life help other lives it touches by the way."

—Anonymous

When I was young, one of my favorite past times was pretending to be a superhero. Being Asian growing up, I had a lot of opportunities at the dinner table. All I had to do was take a few chopsticks and put them between my fingers, and bam, I was Wolverine.

I even made up my own superheroes: one was a wizard with a laundry basket and lid as his super weapon. I remember I would use the lid to create an indentation in my carpet, and then call upon the forces of darkness, essentially demons (I'm glad my parents never knew about this) to do my "bidding." Fortunately, for my school and classmates these demons were meant to fight evil and bad guys.

When I got into the world of Dungeons and Dragons, I created my own character, Rathomar D'Angel, the angel of wrath (sometimes I even scare myself).

Rathomar was a dark elf. Dark elves were black skinned and lived in caves. When I, Rathomar, was just a baby, my family along with his body guards (of course I was royalty) were going for a walk in the caves and ran into a monster which unfortunately killed everyone except me.

As this monster was about to eat me, another group of elves who lived on the mountain and were doing their routine rounds stumbled upon us, killing the monster and saving me.

Not knowing what to do with this baby, they took me back. And by good fortune and the compassion of the high-elf royal family, I was adopted and raised in the tradition, culture, and education of the high elves. I was able to fight like a high elf and perform the magic of a high elf, but because of my heritage as a dark elf, I could also do "darker" and stronger magic.

I, Rathomar, grew up to be a powerful warrior mage, fighting evil in my continual search for power, learning new spells, and acquiring magical items.

Okay, so your imagination may not be as wild or fanatic as mine. You probably never dreamed of or even thought about half the stuff I did, but that doesn't mean you can't relate does it?

Superheroes are a big thing, it seems, nowadays

Wolverine, X-Men, Thor, Ironman, the Avengers, the Defenders, the list goes on. Nerd or not, male or female, old or young, we all seem to have a fascination with superheroes. I honestly can't believe how many superhero movies, sequels, and television shows have been made and generated millions. The superhero media industry is just crazy.

Or is it?

I think we are all born with a desire. A desire that transcends age, gender, race, and culture for a superhero, to be a superhero, and to have superpowers. We desire to be saved and to help save.

We desire to have influence as we already discussed. We desire, at the most basic level, to make stuff. To make a difference. To change, to shape, to transform something or somebody.

From books titled *Wired to Create*, to Canadian much music's slogan "Made to Make," to memes saying "I just wanna drink coffee and make stuff," our human desire, our basic human need is screaming to do something, to make something.

I'm not referring to something grandiose or existential; I'm not saying that we all want to change the world, protect it, or save it. But I do think that all of us want our lives to matter and we all choose to do that in some way, in the way we've been taught, or the way we know how.

In the last chapter, I argued that we desire influence, to have a meaningful impact on others. How we exert influence is through power.

What do you think of when you hear the word power? What do you feel?

Power is a strange word. We can get excited and curious when it is preceded by the word super. And we can feel fear when it is in the wrong hands.

Whether it is super or not, power is simply the ability to exert influence—be it physical, emotional, spiritual, or social influence—upon another person or people. We all have it. Some of us more than others, but we all have it. We all have the ability to do stuff to another person, for better or for worse.

Power, therefore, is the ability to make, break, or take.

Whether it be family units, governments, buildings, businesses, or whatever, these things, concepts, and structures are all created and leveraged for the good of us as a society and of us individually. The sad reality, however, is that when we talk about power, we often think about how it has been and is abused.

We do not live in a perfect world. We don't live in a world where all of us, all the time, are making good and beautiful things in the world. I don't need to go into any detail into this. We live in a broken world and that results in broken people, businesses, governments, and people groups using their power for their own advantage and at the expense of others. What is an intended act of creation, turns into an act of theft and destruction.

The creation, theft, and destruction of value.

Ultimately we either make value, take value, or break value.

Make

In an ideal world, value is only made. Everything that we do in the world, in public and in private, ultimately leads to the benefit and flourishing of not only ourselves but of everyone.

We say everything in a way that builds everyone up for the better. That doesn't mean we only give superficial compliments to one another but we say everything in love and in truth. As a result, we are encouraged, even when it is difficult and hard to hear, to become our better self.

We conduct business where everyone comes out better and a winner. From the board, to the CEO, to the employees, and to the clients, everyone, every single person involved, comes out better.

Fast Fashion according to the documentary *True Cost* is the second greatest contributor to pollution after greenhouse gases. In an ideal world, shopping at Zara, H&M, and Forever 21 would result in not only the saving of our money and the creation of jobs for university students, but also the flourishing of the environment and the people who made our clothes. Organics are recycled and turned into our t-shirt. Factory workers are provided a decent wage and work environment where they can laugh, take coffee breaks, and love the work they do.

To make value is to ultimately express and create truth, goodness, and beauty without a cost.

Take

In saturated markets, however, there is very little room for growth. We don't need to buy more toilet paper, nor can we be convinced that we need more. Unless they team up with the food industry and put laxatives into everything, toilet paper companies are forced to compete against one another for a stagnant market.

All the advertising and marketing done by toilet paper companies is simply to keep their existing customers, or take them from another competitor. And there is nothing wrong with that. It's probably why toilet paper gets softer and softer. If there was no competition, and we had only one toilet paper company, our toilet paper would probably still feel like sandpaper. Thank you, capitalism.

In the real world, however, most things come at a cost.

At what cost did we get this new toilet paper? Though they made a new toilet paper that's softer and stronger than the competitor, how did they do this? What if they tested their toilet paper on innocent babies who had to be wiped more times than they should and got a rash? What if in the process of making softer toilet paper, horrible chemicals were used and then poured into the sea or the lands of people in 3rd world countries? Though we certainly gained from this, is it possible that we simply took something from the disadvantaged and the world?

Was value truly made or was it simply taken?

Break

There's making, taking, and then there's breaking.

To break is the most heinous of acts. The most useless and meaningless of all acts. It's the bullying of another person. The use of unnecessary hurtful language. Vandalism.

We can make value, take value, and then we can break value.

To break value creates absolutely nothing good or beautiful in the world.

Name calling, gossiping, slandering, littering. When we participate in these, we break value in the life of society and the lives of people.

It may make the offender feel good, better, even superior for a moment, but the feeling is fleeting and, ultimately, leaves the world in a worse off place than before it happened.

My point is simple: we have power.

Power to do things.

Things to people and to the world.

Things that make value, take value, or break the value in and of the world.

What you do matters. What all of us do matters. For better and for worse.

Power for Good

However, power, for all its side effects and imperfections, is ultimately good. Power is not something to be scared of, nor is it something to hate. The problem is that power has been mishandled, misused, and abused. And when we think of good power, primarily in the stories of superheroes with super powers, it is used purely to prevent and protect. Their powers are rarely, if ever, used for redemption and creation.

Bad power is always pro-active. It's always seeking to harm others. But good power seems to always be reactive, always reacting to the forces of evil and rarely, if ever, seeking to make lives better. To be fair though, that would make an uninteresting and boring story. The Avengers fighting aliens in NYC is going to make more money than if they used their powers to feed the poor or build an orphanage.

And as a result, we rarely think well of power, seek power, or even use our own power.

In the stories in which power is wielded in the attempt for good, it certainly does not last long.

In the Lord of the Rings, the humans, elves, and dwarves receive powerful rings with which they were able to do great and good things. The power, however, ultimately corrupts them. As the popular proverb goes, "Power corrupts and absolute power corrupts absolutely."

Tony Stark, despite being the noble Iron Man, defender of the human race, is constantly tripped by his ego and ambition. Seeking for what we can only assume to be good intentions, he ultimately ends up creating the entire problem of the story. As the other popular proverb goes, "The road to hell is paved with good intentions."

Walter White tries to provide for his family, but ultimately goes crazy.

Ok. Sure these are fictional examples. But let's look on the news and see all the people across the globe doing ridiculous things in the name of good. I don't even need to name anyone for you to know this is true.

No wonder power has such a bad rep.

But let me quote someone who I think will make it all better. One man who exerted much power. Someone who made value.

"Power, properly understood, is the ability to achieve purpose. It is the strength required to bring about social, political, or economic changes. In this sense power is not only desirable but necessary in order to implement the demands of love and justice. One of the greatest problems of history is that the concepts of love and power are usually contrasted as polar opposites. Love is identified with a resignation of power and power with a denial of love. What is needed is a realization that power without love is reckless and abusive and that love without power is sentimental and anemic. Power at its best is love implementing the demands of justice. Justice at its best is love correcting everything that stands against love."—Martin Luther King Jr

Power, properly wielded, properly used is power with love.

Martin Luther King Jr. had a good life. He could have decided not to have a dream. Not to share his dream. Not to stand up against injustice. To run away, hide, and give up when his house was bombed and his family was attacked. He could have, but he didn't.

Mother Teresa had immense power over the lepers of India. She could have left. She could have kept her distance. But she didn't.

Every parent has power over their child. They can choose to forget and neglect their child. To sleep in, to ignore their cry. But they do not.

The greatest people in the world are those who are greatly aware of their power and who handle it with great responsibility.

We all know with great power comes great responsibility. But we often forget or miss that we all already have great power and, therefore, a great responsibility.

Whether you choose to or not, you influence the people in your life and the world around you. You are the boss of your life, and you will impact your employees and clients.

Summary

- We all have power.

- The power to make, break, or take value.

- Power has been wielded in the past to cause great damage but also great good.

- Power is best used with love.

Part 2: With Great Responsibility Should Come Great Power

> "Power, properly understood, is the ability to achieve purpose.
> It is the strength required to bring about social, political, or economic
> changes. In this sense power is not only desirable but necessary
> in order to implement the demands of love and justice."
>
> —Martin Luther King
>
> "I am of the opinion that my life belongs to the whole
> community, and as long as I live, it is my privilege to do
> for it whatever I can. I want to be thoroughly used up
> when I die. For the harder I work the more I live."
>
> —George Bernard Shaw

It is not enough to simply say that you have power and, therefore, should be more responsible.

You are responsible and, therefore, should seek more power.

Since power is essentially good and can be used for good, it is a good thing to want to obtain power. So how do we get power? Let us first attempt to define power in a bit more detail.

The 5 levels of Power

John Maxwell is best known for his contribution to business and leadership thinking. His books, *The 21 Irrefutable Laws of Leadership* and *The 21 Indispensable Qualities of a Leader*, continue to be one of the most referred to books on leadership and influence.

For anyone skeptical of any sort of list or leadership "guru," trust me as a fellow skeptic that Maxwell's insights are valuable.

In his book *The 5 Levels of Leadership*, Maxwell presents a hierarchy of qualities that provide and describe the ways in which we lead, or in our language, the ways in which we use power.

Position / Rights: People follow you because they have to.
Permission / Relationships: People follow because they want to.
Production / Results: People follow you because of what you have done for the organization.
People Development / Reproduction: People follow because of what you have done for them.
Pinnacle / Respect: People follow you because of who you are and what you represent.

Whether we are talking about leadership, the leading of others, power, or the ability to affect influence, Maxwell's principles provide a helpful framework in understanding power.

For most of our lives, the stories we were told suggest that those with the most power are those in high positions.

Be it political figures or powerful fighters, power is always perceived through the lens of might and exerted through a position: political or superhuman. Power is always viewed in the framework that those who are physically strong or in a position of strength hold the power over those who are physically weak or in lower positions.

We do what we are told at work because we are told by our boss, not because we like them or respect them, but because we want to keep our jobs.

Is power really just about strength? Position?

For the love of God, I hope not.

Power is so much more than simply a position or the having of a "power" in the political to the "super" sense.

Your power is your being. Your essence. Everything that makes you you is your power.

You are your greatest power.

What I appreciate about Maxwell's teaching and reflections is that no one needs to have anything to have power. You don't need a position to have power. You could simply be well liked, loved, and respected. That is more than enough power than most of us truly know what to do with.

There are many great resources in the world that can help you discover your power and how to leverage it for good, giving you more depth and insight than I have room for here. I explore the two resources which I have found to be most helpful and fulfilling in my own life in chapter 6. Right now I will simply touch on the different ways in which we can think about approaching, and applying our power and how we can affect the world.

Culture

Have you ever walked into a room where everyone was the same, and yet different from you? It's one of the weirdest, most awkward feeling you can have.

Being around attractive, well-to-do, extroverted white people makes me really uncomfortable. Okay, basically being in any group setting where I'm the minority makes me uncomfortable.

Chances are you probably hang out with people who are like you. Whether it's people of the same race, socio-economic bracket, way of life, you name it, let's be real, we like being around people who are like us. And I'm not saying there is anything inherently wrong with that.

The problem, however, is that there is power in numbers, and like all power, it can be used for good or for ill.

When I go to work or when I go to a party and all the white guys are talking about sports, hiking, and camping, I am powerless, and they are in power. I can't change the conversation, and I can't add anything to the conversation. I am left completely powerless to the choice of the majority group to decide whether or not they would like to change the topic to something that I could contribute to.

In the business world, women are forced to work harder, look better, and do everything better than the average man only to receive "equal" opportunity. They are not able to change their wages because everyone who can is a man.

Not to get too political, but we can agree there is a problem, however small you want to call it and as little as you want to acknowledge it, with race. We want to build walls and send people back. We discourage or have been discouraged from interracial dating and marriages. We all like and try to preserve ourselves, our comfort, our status, and our way of life from the outsider.

Whenever you're the majority demographic, in race, gender, income-bracket, age, religion or anything else, you have power. You don't need to be a white supremacist to have unfair and unpositive feelings towards immigrants, the First Nations people, or the Chinese that are buying up all "our" land.

Character

When we think about powerful people, we often think about people without a heart. People who are ruthless, people who only care about the bottom line, and people who really don't give a rip about other people. And though there are, unfortunately, a lot of people like that, other types of people have power too.

Martin Luther King Jr., Mother Teresa, Gandhi all show that power doesn't necessarily need to come from a position. That there is power in character. That there is power in being a good human being. There is power when people stand up for things they believe in.

Martin Luther King Jr. was inspired by the non-violent actions of Gandhi who was inspired by Jesus in the Bible, and so he took on the same posture in the Civil Rights movement.

Good people and good lives inspire others to live similar lives. There is great power in being good.

Words

"Sticks and stones may break my bones but words can never hurt me."

A phrase that we would tell our bullies to fake them into thinking they were not hurting and bullying us. This statement alone though reveals just how false it is. Words matter. They either build up or break down. Words have power.

Every day you have the ability, you have the power, to either bring someone up or bring someone down. You can either compliment or criticize. Commend or condemn. Bless or belittle.

I heard somewhere that the typical child receives ten criticisms for every one compliment in their childhood. No wonder we're so screwed up.

And our words are not just a way to wield power, but a way to gain and lose power.

If I say wise, loving, and good things to you all the time, I'm going to have more power over you in the long run. Referring back to Maxwell's 5 Levels of Leadership, the more you like me and respect me, the more power or capital I have with you.

In the same respect, if I put you down all the time, call you names, criticize every little thing that you do, I'm going to diminish whatever respect you had for me or relationship we have and ultimately lose power.

Words have power. To build or break value and to build or break our ability to.

Money

As someone who cares a lot about how he looks, I spend more than some on the maintenance of my appearance. Over the last eight months, however, I have been personally convicted of the relationship between fashion and injustice in the world and my implicit role in it.

I am not saying large global fashion companies are evil. They do provide a sense of beauty in the world and jobs for university students and other people. They do do good in that sense. But the reality is that many people are abused and forced into horrible work conditions to provide me the luxury of the most stylish and affordable clothing. As someone with an Asian heritage, I can't help but think my foreparents, and even myself, could be working and living in a situation that many are in right now.

How can I comply with a system that is perpetuating the bondage and enslavement of a potential life my family and I might have lived?

Does this mean I now buy all my clothes second hand? No way.

As I have thought about it, I have decided to, as best as I can, only give my money towards brands and companies that I believe are not simply taking value, but actually creating value. I unsubscribed from the many brands that I once loved receiving promotional and sales emails from.

I now without any guilt, buy from a brand called Everlane, which is one company among a few, committed to some form of sustainable fashion and business. Though they are not perfect, they seem, by every measure, to be doing more good than harm in the world.

On Black Friday of 2016, instead of having the traditional sale to generate more revenue, they had a campaign to raise funds for a cause. On the homepage of their website, they told the world that if they could generate

$125,000 in revenue for the day, they would have enough profits to be able to provide 8,000 road helmets for their Vietnamese factory workers.

As they explained in their promotional video, most people commute and drive their children around by scooters. However, the use of a helmet is optional and an expense most are unable to make. As a result, people every day are involved in motor vehicle accidents and often sustain injury.

As an act to protect and serve their Vietnamese employees, Everlane invited their customers to shop for a cause. Everlane raised more than enough funds halfway into the day.

With Everlane, I can buy clothes without guilt. Though it may be somewhat naive, I like to think that in my purchasing, wearing, and instagramming of my Ethical clothing, I am doing some good in the world. It might not be a lot, but it is good. I'm using the little power that I have, in the disposable money that I possess, and using it for the development and flourishing of others. In this case, everyone wins.

Do I pay a bit more? Yes.

Does that extra bit more that I do pay get multiplied exponentially in benefits for the less fortunate? I think so.

Is it worth it then? Heck to the yes.

How we spend our money is how we use our power. And no matter how little or how much we have, we have a responsibility.

A responsibility not only on how we spend, but also a responsibility to be informed.

Education and Knowledge

I might be stating the obvious, but knowledge, education, is power.

For parents with young children, probably one of their most important goals, other than helping their child learn to walk, is ensuring they can read. Literacy is considered the #1 deciding factor for a child's growth and success in life.

The world would be a better place if people just read more. It wouldn't be a perfect place by any means, but it would be better. If we all read books like Dale Carnegie's *How to Win Friends and Influence People*, Susan Cain's *Quiet*, and Brené Brown's *The Gifts of Imperfection* and *Daring Greatly*, I think the world would definitely be a better place.

Gandhi read the Bible and was inspired to follow the words and actions of Jesus, taking non-compliant and non-violent action. The dude's not even a Christian, but he chose to read something, expanded his mind, exerted much power, and transformed the world.

And if we all read a little bit more on how to help people, just anything, we will have more power.

Knowledge is power. Whether it's knowledge about science, English, history, people, yourself, whatever, you got power and you can get more of it.

Read. Watch a documentary. Watch a Ted Talk. Take an online course. Take a class at your local college.

Just do something that expands your brain.

Experience and Wisdom

With the gaining of knowledge, we then have more power and a greater capacity for influence. However, it is said that knowledge is the possession of information, but wisdom is the application of knowledge.

When you actually apply what you learned in the books, you become wiser. And the wiser you become, the more power you thus possess.

Did you know that in some parts of the country, you can actually hire or arrange a senior citizen to play with your child? And did you know that there are people, ridiculously unqualified people, who are making exorbitant amounts of money to be "mentors" to others?

We have a parenting crisis right now. A mentorship issue.

If you have life experience, a story, and have learned from it, you have power. People are craving the knowledge, wisdom, and experience of people who have gone before them and learned from it.

The beauty and exciting thing about age and experience being power is that you keep getting more! That is if you learn from it.

Every day you make choices. Some good and some not so good. Whenever you reflect on them and learn from them, you gain wisdom and therefore power. How awesome and easy is that?

Summary

- Your power doesn't have to come from a place of authority or position.

- The pinnacle of power is where people respect you because of your character and how you have lived.

- You can express and produce power through your culture, character, words, money, education, and experience.

CHAPTER 5

Establish Your Principles:
You Are What You Believe

Part 1: Values, and Worldview

> "A belief is not merely an idea the mind possesses;
> it is an idea that possesses the mind."
>
> —Robert Oxton Bolton

> "Strong hope is a much greater stimulant of life
> than any single realized joy could be."
>
> —Friedrich Nietzche

A few months ago my friend, Jack, and I were having a conversation about traveling: where we would love to go and what we would love to do. For myself, I'd love to travel to New York, Boston, Melbourne, and Sydney, drinking coffee, and eating brunch. For Jack, he would love to go to

Australia and do all those things, but what would really make his trip is getting laid.

The more notable thing, though, is that my friend, Jack, has a girlfriend. He, however, believes that whatever happens outside the continent, stays outside the continent. Once you cross the ocean, everywhere apparently is Vegas. Think what you may of Jack and his beliefs or morals, the simple fact is he believes one thing and some of us may believe another. And what you believe, what your principles are, determine the choices you make today and tomorrow.

The last component to discovering our true self and living our best life is to establish our principles.

Don't get me wrong. Before we continue, I must say in no way do I approve of my friend's desires or perspective on how a committed relationship should be conducted. However, who am I to say his thinking is wrong either? On what grounds or principles do I base my thoughts and judgments? Who or what has determined, what I will assume most of us believe, that cheating is wrong?

For the unspiritual, it's science. Science suggests that committed relationships lead to healthy marriages, which leads to healthy families, which leads to healthy children, and which ultimately leads to a healthier society. Some "scientists" however would argue that monogamy is impractical and unnatural.

For the spiritual, it's God. People make a sacred and solemn vow before their God and community and promise to remain faithful for the sake of their faith and community.

For everyone in between, it's a complex mixture of science, spirituality, and their society. One might say: "I don't necessarily believe in God, but I do believe that there is some sort of greater power or truth in the world.

Cheating is wrong, yes, because it hurts the children and ultimately society, but it is also wrong because it just is, and I believe it even though other societies would say otherwise."

Whatever philosophy each of us holds however, we have all come to one and need to recognize how we got there and how to further establish what is true, good and beautiful. Some read ancient texts, others listen to thought leaders, my friend Justin, takes MDMA and shrooms.

So, who determines what's right and wrong? Well, you do. Each of us look to the opinions and teachings of others, be it our parents, a culture or tradition, and take it for what it is, or modify it.

I'm not trying to push any particular religion or philosophy of life on you, but what I am pushing is that you do have one whether you have thought about it or not. And whatever philosophy you do have, you need to clarify, solidify, and let it lead your life.

Assuming you agree that cheating, particularly marital infidelity, is in the most general terms wrong, you must know why you actually believe that. From the religious to the atheist, your mixture of principles will determine how each person approaches and understands each situation. For example, is cheating wrong for the wife if the husband already is? What if instead he's just away a lot for work, trying to provide more than enough for his family, and she's feeling neglected, lonely, and miserable? Or what if the children are grown up, and the both of them have naturally drifted away over the years? What if it's consensual?

Is marital fidelity important because people made vows and keeping their promises no matter what is important? Or is it important because both people's overall happiness is important?

Though none of us ever plan to find ourselves in a less than ideal and perfect marriage, how do we, or how will we, determine how to handle our marriage and situation when we are in the thick of it? No one plans on cheating aside from Jack and the, hopefully, rare few. But it happens more than we would expect and know of. Can we really afford to believe we are immune to the complexities of life and the world?

If you want to really live out your best life, you need to clarify and solidify your principles so you can stand strong when the wind and waves eventually come. What exactly do you believe and why? What is good? What is true? What is beautiful?

If you can't clearly answer and define these, life will be difficult to say the least. You'll be running a marathon in the desert not knowing which star to follow. You'll be sailing the open seas without a compass. You get my drift (no pun intended). Without concrete beliefs, you won't have clear direction. Without a solid foundation, you won't be able to build a solid framework to build your life upon.

You need to know what is true, good, and beautiful in order to live your life with as little confusion and with as much clarity as possible. God knows life is confusing enough as it is.

We all have different opinions on what is true, good, and beautiful, don't we? We can agree on big picture stuff like peace and love, but the details, definitions, and implications are quite blurry and left to interpretation. And we only agree to that because you and I have been influenced by modern western culture. Peace and love for all are certainly not the good, true, and beautiful for political dictators and sex-traffickers.

For me, personally, I think one of the most beautiful things in this world is a multiracial family, with adopted children, living in the city, all dressed like a boss. Basically Angelina Jolie and Brad Pitt when they were together. I still miss Brad and Jen though.

You might not agree with me, however. The most beautiful type of family for you might be two people who grew up in the same hometown and who had three to five children by the time they were thirty.

I'm not suggesting that either of us think the others view is ugly or not good.

I'm simply saying that beauty is both objective and subjective.

What?

All loving families are beautiful, but most people do have a particular *image* of the kind of family they will one day have. I've been on enough dating sites to know race, height, and body type are significant factors for people. Thinking something is beautiful does not take away the beauty from something else.

Because of our differing views on the *ideal* image of the family, you and I, should consequently make decisions in our dating based off this image. For example, someone who wishes to live in the suburbs and have a large family should probably find a partner that desires that same life. I recently met a woman who wants to move to Israel and work with people towards peace and reconciliation. That's amazing! But I do not think that is the life for me and therefore why nothing happened beyond making an amazing friend.

Knowing your truth, your goodness, and your beauty is not only important for your own happiness and future, but it is also for your loved ones.

If I, hypothetically speaking, believe that marriage is simply a man-made institution from religion and imposed by government, and thus marital fidelity is fluid and contextual, then I, at the very least, should look for and ultimately marry someone of the same disposition.

If we both fall out of our feelings for one another, then we can peaceably agree to separate and work together as individuals who share the same children.

But if I married someone who very much believed in the sanctity of marriage and the promise of "til death do us part," and I knew we had differing beliefs, our divorce would be much more complicated. She would feel hurt and betrayed. She would suggest couples therapy and to work it out. She might even believe we should just stay married and go through the motions for the sake of our children.

But since marriage is simply a religious and institutional contraption to me, then I'll believe our marriage has simply run its course and inevitably not fight as hard or at all.

Establishing your principles enables you to possess a more defined path to walk.

We agree that whether it's adopted or biological children, both are beautiful because there is love. But the families we imagine and seek are influenced by what we believe to be more beautiful.

Truth, goodness, and beauty are, in a macro way, relative. Relative only because as finite human beings, none of us can determine what is the best. You would agree that I can't tell you the exact kind of family you should have. But you would also agree that I can "tell" you and the world that every family should have love.

Where we would begin to verge into differences of opinion would be the definition and the practical implications of love.

One form of parenting may believe that to love their child means to seek their material welfare and stability. Whereas another form may believe that to love their child means to seek their happiness and independence.

Love, as universally true, good, and beautiful as it may be, is in a way "relative." There is no one way to *do* it.

To be our best means that we pursue and live out what we believe to be true, good, and beautiful. We live with integrity. We live according to our values. Our principles.

However, our principles should not be defined and determined on our own.

Take my friend Jack's truth that "whatever happens over the ocean, stays over the ocean." I'll bet you would disagree with his statement. But who are you to judge? On what objective grounds are you able to say that you know what is right? Many men cheat on their wives without guilt because, in their opinion, loving their wife means providing a financially comfortable and prosperous life. Or they might even believe they owe nothing to their wives, least of all fidelity.

Or take the Alt-Right/Nazi/White-Supremacist movement for example. They believe very strongly in principles that the majority of us do not agree with. How would you argue with someone from that movement, on the invalidity of their position?

You can't. And that's the problem.

They believe in certain principles and we believe in certain principles, but we all have different frameworks or worldviews, on which these principles are built upon.

We can all agree that the value of the flourishing of a people group is not a universal value. The welfare of African-Americans, immigrants/refugees, and First Nations people is not the primary concern for the general population.

RYAN LUI

And therefore here lies the challenge and hard work of establishing our principles: we can't establish our principles individually or even collectively. Jack and the Alt-Right movement are both examples of people who established their principles on their own.

We can't say in one breath that goodness, truth, and beauty are relative. That my truth is mine and your truth is yours and then criticize another person for their beliefs even if you disagree with them.

Either truth, goodness, and beauty does not exist, or there is a universal truth, goodness, and beauty in the world which we have to discover intelligently.

To be our best, we need to have a clear set of beliefs about what is good, true, and beautiful.

But we also need to fact-check them.

We need to converse with people who think differently than us. We need to learn about the history of our thoughts and culture. We need wisdom.

All of us are subject to pride. We are all subject to believe we hold the knowledge of the universe even when the rest of history and the world would disagree with us. So much of American politics is fueled by people and parties unwilling to budge on their position and listen to their opponent.

I wonder how much conflict we create in our lives because we, too, are unwilling to listen and dialogue with others.

We are fallible: subject to error.

The problem with all self-help books, including my own; religious texts; and anything else that may encourage a person to live a certain way is that they should all be read in a community of people. Both like-minded and different.

This is how we avoid cults and fanatics.

Every book can be and has been misinterpreted, and so we must all be wise to not make the same mistake.

Determining what is universally good, true, and beautiful, however, is way too big and philosophical of a topic for us to get into.

So, we're just going to start with you, right here and now: what is the most good, true and beautiful for you and how is that guiding your life?

What is your worldview? How do you see and interpret the world? What is the world and why is it here? I recognize again that this is complicated stuff. Stuff we don't normally, if ever, think or talk about. But I believe it's important.

Like real important.

Life or death important.

Your worldview, how you understand the world and its meaning, is absolutely critical to discovering the life you are to live. It determines the daily and big decisions of your life.

William Wilberforce believed in the dignity and inherent value of every person based on his faith and therefore dedicated his life to the banishment of slavery in the United Kingdom. Mother Teresa believed that the most undesirable people of the world, are equally deserving of love, compassion, and human touch based upon her belief that there is a God who commands the people who believe in him to serve and love the poor.

Martin Luther King Jr., Nelson Mandela, and Gandhi, to name a few more, are all people who lived by principles which they believed to be true, contrary to the public, yet were affirmed by their faith and soul. They believed in an alternative world that their current world did not inhabit, and they believed that it was their purpose to be involved somehow.

Presently I think of Elon Musk, who despite the financial risks and losses, is pursuing something greater than most can even fathom.

Your worldview, in essence, is what you believe about the world: where the world is, where the world should end up, and what your role (if any) is in taking the world a step closer to that end. If the world is on a journey, the questions you should ask are:

1) What should the world be like?

2) What is it honestly right now?

3) Where is the world headed?

4) What part do I play in making the world closer to my answer to question 1?

This book is ultimately about being the person you were born to be and living out the life you were made to live. It is about purpose in the broadest sense of the word. It goes beyond what we should do to who we should be.

We could also use the word calling which is becoming more popular. However, as Professor Os Guinness, descendant of the maker of Guinness beer, so poignantly says in his book, *The Call*, a calling implies that there is a caller. You can't' have a calling, you can't be called, unless someone or something is calling you.

Going back to passion and how love is both relational and eternal, who (of whom you love) or what (that is true, good, and beautiful) is calling you?

Summary

- Your principles are what you believe to be true, good, and beautiful.

- Each of us believe differently as to what is true, good, and beautiful.

- Some principles are a matter of opinion; others are a matter of truth or fact.

- Just because we believe something, doesn't necessarily mean it is true; therefore, we must check our beliefs with others.

- The collective framework of your beliefs is called your worldview.

Part 2: Direction to Discernment

> "The chief cause of failure and unhappiness is trading what you want most for what you want right now."
>
> —Zig Ziglar

> "In matters of principle, stand like a rock; in matters of taste, swim with the current."
>
> —Thomas Jefferson

So you know your principles. You have this list—which is probably pretty long if you think about all the things you believe are important, all that is true, good and beautiful in the world—and now you have to prioritize them.

You need to create some sort of plan or framework in which you will live out your principles because, sooner or later, they will compete.

In pursuit of my business degree, I learned the necessity of performing what is called a "cost-benefit analysis." In business, we are always making decisions. Decisions that always come with a cost. If we hire more servers, we are going to have less money for new plates and for the future renovation. What's more important: fast service or a beautiful atmosphere? Although you shouldn't treat life as a giant business with everything and every person as either profit or loss, you do need to think about what is important and what isn't as much.

Whenever you make a decision, you are choosing between multiple decisions or options. If you choose A, you aren't choosing B.

In business generally, the bottom line is profits. Some businesses, however, are choosing to put people over profits. Social enterprise or multiple-bottom-line businesses are becoming increasingly popular.

I get my coffee from a company I love called Level Ground. They are a for-profit company, and yet also prioritize people. One of their products is dried mangoes. They squeeze out the juice, dry the mangoes, and do whatever else is required. However, instead of simply wasting the juices, they collect the juices, bottle it up, and give it to their employees to take home to their families. Level Ground's factories operate in some of the poorest places of the world, and they are committed to the flourishing of the people they employ, their families, and their community.

Level Ground knows their principles, knows their priorities, and lives them out accordingly. Their business is most likely more complicated, but in the grey and messiness of it all, they achieve their greater purpose and receive a greater joy.

As complicated as business is, our lives are infinitely more so. And if it's important for a business to sort their priorities, how much more would it be for us?

You need to know your priorities.

Priorities

We all have them. We just might not be able to articulate them and make informed decisions from them.

Ever made a mistake? Did something you regretted? Did you forget your principles? Probably not. You most likely shifted around your priority list in the moment only to regret it later.

Don't worry, we all do it.

At least I do . . .

What are your priorities? How are you going to make a decision between two good, true, and beautiful things? How do you choose between happiness and fidelity? How do you discern what you are called to do in a given situation?

Life is complicated enough amidst all the principles and options we have. We need to further uncomplicate and simplify it by prioritizing them. Profits or people?

Apparently, Steve Jobs wasn't the greatest or nicest boss; he certainly wasn't a people person, in that he didn't care about work life balance. The first few generations of iPhones reportedly were manufactured by Chinese citizens in slave-like conditions. But because of his priorities, we have entered into a new era of life.

Am I defending the decisions of Apple? By no means. I am saying, however, that they clearly knew their priorities and made the logical decisions in accordance with it.

Some helpful resources that I have found are Michael Hyatt's *Life Planner*. You can get the ebook for free on his website michaelhyatt.com. Though it's an extremely simple practice, simply writing down a list of your principles and trying to list them in order of importance can be very illuminating and helpful.

BEING IS GREATER THAN DOING

Although this is a classic which many people around the world have already read and summarized, Steven Covey's *The 7 Habits of Highly Effective People* is a must read for everyone.

The most helpful and most widely referred to of his seven habits is his "Important vs Urgent" matrix. Basically, in life, every decision we make (which there are a ton of everyday) has a certain level of importance and a certain level of urgency.

Some things need to get done like right now. But not all of these things, however, are that important and should be given your full attention or time.

Covey helps us realize that we spend a lot of time, too much time, on things that fall in the urgent but not important category and things that fall in the non-urgent and not-important category: Netflix, errands, emails, and social media. These things are all to various degrees things we don't have to do right away.

What happens, in the non-principled and not-prioritized life, is that the important yet non-urgent things like saving your money or reading books for personal development are often neglected. Sure, they're important, but there's not an immediate negative consequence for not doing them now (or even ever).

Go out on the town with the boys or stay in and save $100 out of the $100,000 that I need to buy a house?

I think I'll just spend that $100 and worry about that $100,000 tomorrow.

Sometimes, we need to do that. No one likes a stick-in-the-mud who stays in and saves every day and every night. That person has no friends or will soon lose them all. The problem, however, is that most of us (myself included) think in the now. We intellectually know saving is important, that we should save for our retirement, spouse or children, but what "real" effect is there in spending a Benjamin or two tonight?

We need to be aware of what's important and what is urgent. What is not important and what is not-urgent. Everything is on a spectrum and every decision we have to make can have an infinite set of values (e.g., Importance 5 and Urgency 2 or Importance 5.9 and urgency 1.8) If only it were as easy as assigning a numerical value to every principle, then just looking it up every time we make a decision and then doing whatever is listed.

If only.

We need to prioritize our principles in order to have a sense of direction.

But in order to do this, we also need wisdom.

We need discernment.

Discernment

I heard recently that Elon Musk, founder of Tesla, said that the greatest need for world security and peace is the banning of war-designed artificial intelligence. If you've watched any post-apocalyptic movie where robots take over the world, you'll know that the robots were always originally created for the common good. But out of the programming of these robots, it is always eventually deduced that the world would be better off without humanity.

We are not robots nor should we live like them. We have principles, and we should have priorities, but we should not live by them as a program.

Or else you may become Skynet.

BEING IS GREATER THAN DOING

I am indebted to Peter Scazerro's *Emotionally Healthy Spirituality*, in which he refers to the psychological term of "differentiation." Differentiation is the ability to clearly define one's life values and goals in life. When a person is differentiated, they are not silenced by the voice of haters; they do not take the life of another, nor do they run away in fear of the challenges and battles of pursuing their purpose.

In Scazerro's book, Peter takes the famous and widely popular story of David and Goliath to expand on the idea of differentiation, which I will attempt to summarize now.

Once upon a time, Israel, which we will call America in our story, had a king named Saul who was at war with the neighboring country, which we will call Canada. In ancient times, it was the expectation that the king would fight in the war for the people. In their situation, Saul was the king of the Jewish people who was believed to be appointed by God to be their king. So even though he's an important dude, he's in there with the people, fighting alongside them, not like the president who just makes decisions from his far and safe castle.

In this certain war with Canada, however, Saul decides for whatever reason to stay in his castle and let the people fight without him. Unfortunately, Canada summons their top fighter Goliath, this monstrous nine-foot man who is their super fighter/champion, and challenges the other army, America, to produce a warrior to fight Goliath to decide the outcome of the war once and for all.

As the army of America is trembling in fear, not knowing what to do or who will fight, a boy named David shows up to the battlefield. Like any annoying teenager, he starts speaking without thinking about the consequences. He says things like, "Why isn't anyone fighting? We are the people of God? Why should we be afraid? How dare Canada stand up to us; we should obliterate them!"

As you can imagine, this might ruffle a few feathers. In fact his brother was there, and said "Yo what the heck David? How dare you say things you have no place to say." (I'm taking some translation liberties)

David, however, keeps mouthing off. "How dare Canada challenge us! We are God's country! We can, should, and will kill em! Let me fight him!"

Eventually, some dude hears him and tells King Saul. Being the scared and weak man he is, Saul agrees to let him fight. So he comes over from his castle to the battlefield to talk to David.

Even though Saul thinks that David won't be able to fight or win, given that he's a scrawny, 13-year-old kid whose only work or battle experience has been shepherding sheep and protecting them from lions and bears, he agrees to letting him fight since no one else is stepping up.

In his best attempt to support David, Saul gives David his own royal armor and weaponry. Just imagine a full suit of super heavy, shiny, golden steel armor. David puts this on and realizes immediately that the armor is too big and too heavy. In Goldilocks' language, the armor was just not right. So David makes the executive decision to take off the armor and fight without it and without Saul's sword. He decides instead to fight with what he knows and what's "proven" to be effective. He fights with no armor and with what he's always fought with: a sling shot.

And as you probably know, David fights the monstrous man, slays Goliath, and wins. America (Israel) 1, Canada 0. Take that Canada. (I'm Canadian if you didn't know, so no disrespect to my fellow countrymen and women)

The moral of the story is not that despite the odds, the small guy can beat the big guy.

In this story, David had three choices and three opportunities to act differently. He could have shut up when his older brother told him to. He could have put on and fought with Saul's armor and weaponry. And he could have ran at the last minute when he saw how scary Goliath really was. The point of this story is that in life you have four choices when making your own life decisions:

1) Shut up, stay quiet, and don't do anything.

2) Go for it, but do it someone else's way. Do it the way everyone has before. Follow someone else's steps and live someone else's life.

3) Run away and go back to doing what you were doing before.

4) Do it the way you were made to.

David believed that this war was important, that the war could and would be won because they were God's people. And he also believed that it was his job, his purpose, to fight and to fight his own way.

As old as this story is, the point is not one bit less important or relevant to us today.

The world, or society, is constantly telling us to shut up and stay put.

To do it their way, to fit in into their way of doing things.

To give up, run away, and do what's safe and easy.

But yo, that's just not good advice.

How do they know what you should do and how to live?

They don't.

Only you know who you are.
Only you can do the hard work of differentiation.
And only you are the one that will walk the road you make.

Haters gonna hate, and there's nothing we can do about that.

But if what you want to do and live by brings truth, goodness, and beauty into the world, who has a right to stop you?

Be the person you were born to be.

Live the life you are supposed to live.

And do it the way that you were meant to do it.

David did, and he slew a giant.

If David's principles were less about honoring God and more about self-preservation, David wouldn't have fought.

If David's principles were less about fighting wisely and more about obeying authority (brother or king), then David would have lost the fight.

David fought because of the direction of his priorities. But he won because of the discernment of his purpose.

David didn't just know what he believed, but he knew who he was.

He lived by principles but acted out of his *power*.

Just because you may live by one principle more strongly in one situation than another does not mean you have betrayed your principles or are living incongruently or hypocritically. Family first doesn't mean always being at home with the children nor does it mean always working to provide for them. A mother isn't only a wife, a mom, or an employee. She is all three.

Though our principles fuel the direction of our life, it is the wise discernment of all our principles together which will determine the living out of our purpose. Our personhood.

Path vs. Purpose

When we think about our purpose, we often in the same breath talk about our path. We use metaphors like life is a journey or life is a marathon, suggesting that there is a path and a goal.

However, I want to share something that really freed me from a lot of unrecognized, unnecessary pressure that I had accumulated.

There is no path. (There is no spoon).

At least, there is no *one* path any of us must live.

When you think of your life's "plan" or "path," this implies that if things do not go according to plan, or if you go off path, then you are essentially living the wrong life or out of alignment to your purpose.

That there is one way, and then there is the highway.

That if you don't live this way, in this way, you are a failure.

That is a lot of freaking pressure.

But as one of my distant mentors and professors taught me in class, "God has a grand purpose for your life, not a narrow plan."

Life, your life, my life, our lives, have a lot more freedom than we have ever been taught or may think.

By definition, if we don't follow the plan, the program, the manual or the instructions, we will build something wrong.

Some things do have an exact plan, an exact manual. For example, if I don't follow the guide or plan that Ikea gives me for building my sofa, I'm most likely going to build an inferior product. But when we apply this to things that don't have an exact plan or manual, we could buckle under the pressure. When we think about our life's plan or path, we can mistakenly think that if we make even the slightest mistake, we will live a life that is inferior.

Whatever your beliefs or worldview is, I hope for your sake you can apply what my professor taught me: Your life has a grand purpose and not a narrow plan.

Take heart that your life and the world will not end if you choose a direction that, in retrospect, didn't lead to everything you had ever hoped and dreamed for. Most decisions rarely, if ever, do.

Live by principles and priorities, but live for a purpose.

Seek direction, but choose by discernment.

Remember, the purpose of life, primarily, is not to do something, but to be somebody.

We are human beings, not human doings.

Whatever you choose to do, whatever path you take, whether optimal or not, when you learn from it, grow from it, and become more of the person you were born to be, then you have fulfilled your purpose. You actually did what you were supposed to.

You became who you were meant to be.

Summary

- In order to live well, we need to not only have a list of principles to live by, but also a set of priorities and ultimately a purpose.

- Life doesn't have a plan or map to go by, nor is it a complete adventure into the unknown.

- Priorities can't be simply decided however, they have to be discerned.

- Discernment requires emotional awareness and wisdom.

- We are human beings, not human doings.

SECTION 3

The Six Practices
to Personhood

CHAPTER 6

Recognize Who You Are

"When the day comes that I must account for my life, I will not be asked: 'Why weren't you Moses?' I was not equipped to be Moses. But I dread the question, 'Why weren't you Zusia?'"

—Rabi Zusia of Anipoli

"Be yourself; everyone else is already taken."

—Oscar Wilde

Now this may be somewhat redundant given everything you've read so far, but it's always worth repeating:

Knowing yourself is really important.

We can't know what to do if we don't know who we are.

The challenge though is that we're complicated.

We are an iceberg where only 10% is visible and the other 90% is submerged beneath the surface. We are deeply complicated beings with often competing thoughts, desires, needs and emotions.

To top that off, our experiences and daily learnings continue to challenge, change, and shape who we are. As we wake up each day to a different world, we also wake up as a different person. We are always changing, and yet we are still the same person.

Man, life is hard.

Change is inevitable; therefore, you must constantly and continually be asking yourself who you are. Constantly recognizing how you are feeling, what you are believing, what you are doing, and how you are changing.

Personal development is so hard because it requires so much self-awareness, in quantity and in quality.

The people who are going to become the person they were born to be and live the life they were meant to live are the people who will overcome this challenge.

They will continually be in the pursuit of self-discovery. Continually asking themselves each and every day "Who am I?"

And as they come closer to an answer, as they come closer to realizing who they truly are, they go and do something about it.

Below are a few ways or tools that I have found to be helpful, if not completely life changing, in helping me discover my authentic self, becoming more confident with who I am, and deepening my sense of my personhood.

StrengthsFinder

About 20 years ago, Gallup Inc. published StrengthsFinder 2.0. A 30-minute assessment that determines your top five strengths out of a total of 34. StrengthsFinder helped me own my power and also embrace my weaknesses/limitations in a way that was life giving and freeing.

Being from an Asian background, I'm often told to focus on my weaknesses. You get all As, and 1 B, and your parents are going to hang you out to dry for that one B rather than celebrate all those As.

With this assessment, however, I more willingly embraced my weaknesses as it revealed to me my strengths. I discovered our greatest weaknesses are simply the natural result or product of our greatest strengths.

According to StrengthsFinder, there are 34 strengths and four distinct categories which these strengths can be somewhat evenly placed. These four categories are execution (the ability to get stuff done), influence (the ability to move and motivate people), relationship building (the ability to connect with people), and strategic thinking (the ability to think well).

When I got my results and worked with a StrengthsFinder coach, I was blown away at how different I am to others and most importantly that it's OK to be different if not good.

My strengths in my layman definition are as follows:

1) Futuristic (Strategic Thinking)—I'm all about the future. I live in the future. I breathe the future. Everything I see and do is in one way or another related to the future, my future, your future, my company's future.

Downside: It's hard for me to think about a plan and to be present.

2) Maximizer (Influence)—Good to great. Go big or go home. These are some of the mottos of my life. I don't do well with average or even good for that matter. If I'm going to do something, I'm going to do it freaking awesomely. If I'm going to work for somebody or work for something, it better be for something big. Everything for me needs to be *legendary*.

Downside: I'm pretty impatient and not the most realistic with resources; I suck at multitasking because it often requires doing a lot of different things fairly well. I can only do one or two things at a time. But if I do them, I'm going to kill them.

3) Significance (Influence)—To be significant is to have lasting and great value to something. A paper cup that held your coffee last week is in the big scheme of things completely insignificant to your life. Your mom or mentor was very significant to your life. With the significance strength, I want to be significant. Now, I think we all want to be significant, none of us want to be a paper coffee cup in the world or in everyone's life, but according to SF and in my own personal experience, I want it a bit more. I don't have to be the center of attention (though I'll never say no to the chance); I just want to know that I had a meaningful contribution, whether to the company, a project, or the lives of my friends and family.

Downside: I'm not a good team player, and I'm highly unmotivated by anything I deem insignificant.

4) Belief (Execution)—It's arguable that our beliefs determine everything. Our beliefs about the world, ourselves, the people around us. If I believe something, whether true or not, I'm going to do something about it. I can be chill about most things, but if you get me started on something I am passionate about or believe in, you better watch out.

Downside: I can be pretty polarizing. There are things that I just believe (usually with good intention and reason) that may cause a lot of conflict between us.

5) Learner (Strategic Thinking)—I like to learn. Specifically, rather, I *need* to learn. If I ever feel stuck in life, I will need to learn something new. Whether that's the newest idea on getting a six pack, the latest diet trend, how to sew, how to make my own rustic looking table, or simply the latest findings on sociology and the human mind, I must learn something. If I don't, I feel dead inside.

Downside: I can get stuck in my head and get distracted from my main priorities.

In summary, I am a future-oriented dreamer who has an insatiable need to learn, motivated by a set of unshakeable values to be my best, and help others live likewise.

Realizing who I am in terms of my strengths and limitations has helped me . . .

Perform better at work.
Own my power.
Embrace my imperfections, weaknesses, and limitations.
Stay humble and grounded, knowing I'm not perfect by any stretch and that I need people.
Be less judgmental.
Appreciate others and their strengths.
Get a clearer picture of what flourishing looks like for me.

And realizing who you are in terms of your strengths and limitations will help you do the same.

Embracing our pain and our limitations is essential to knowing who we are and becoming our best. Yet it is often difficult to embrace our pain, our brokenness and our limitations if we cannot see the silver lining amidst it all. Hopefully StrengthsFinder helps you see the goodness and beauty within you and accept your humanity and limitations.

The Enneagram

The Enneagram is the other "test" that changed my life. These are pretty much the only two tests or profiles that changed my life, so don't worry I don't have any more.

The Enneagram is a nine-type personality profile. Each one of us "major" in one of these personalities, and then "minor" in another. Each personality type has a particular way of looking at and coping with the world.

For myself, I'm a 4 (the Romantic) and then a 3 (The Performer). This affects how I see the meaning of life: to become our true and authentic selves, characterized by being our best.

For the Perfectionist (type 1), their goal is to be morally good. For the Peacemaker (type 9), their goal is to maintain peace in their self, their relationships and in the world. Or for the Enthusiast (type 7), their goal is to be happy. Each of these goals along with the others that I have not mentioned will be influenced by our minor or secondary personality.

If you were to explore the Enneagram in depth, you'll discover your basic desire and fear, how you handle stress, your virtue and vice, and a framework toward emotional and spiritual wholeness. I love it because it uncovers the beauty and potential greatness of every person but also the darkness that lies within each of us.

Because we have all been uniquely made, we each have a unique "best." For the Achiever (type 3), their best will ultimately be becoming a person of achievement but with self-awareness, loyalty, and love. For the Helper (type 2), they will help and love others without any strings attached but also live their own life rather than the one they thought would bring them the love they have for so long desired.

By using the Enneagram, you will recognize the true motivation of your life and a framework to wholeness. You will, at the very least, recognize that other people are different than you and that that is okay. That every human being expresses imperfectly and partially, the good, true, and beautiful of the world.

Realizing who we are and who we are not doesn't only have to be done in the context of personality tests though they are by far the most accessible and objective. I have also found it very helpful to realize that I am the product of my culture.

Culture

You and I are different.

We may be of a different ethnicity, gender, nationality, age, religion, and socio-economic levels to name a few. All of these play a major role in our development, our worldview, and our personality. It's hard to really know how much of us has come from nurture and how much from nature. When we acknowledge the differences in culture and, therefore, the natural differences in people, we are able to get a better sense of who we are in light of who others are and are not.

Yet again I will refer back to the Enneagram and the basic assertion that there are different personalities that are equally good. Just as there is no one better personality, there is no one better culture.

Our Western, Achiever, Type-3 culture that so dominates our perspectives on the meaning of life, our politics, our business practices and relationships, is not superior than the Type-9 culture of gentle and humble living for example. According to the Franciscan priest Richard Rohr, the majority of the non-Western world and humanity untouched by the West, is most likely a type-9 culture.

Recognizing that you and I have in some way been impacted by the Achiever (type 3) personality will help us see that so much of our goals in life have been decided for us. And if we can recognize that some of the goals which we have strived for in life are actually our culture's and not our own, we may begin to be able to recognize who we are not, and ultimately who we are.

Realize who you are not

As I continue to reflect about myself through StrengthsFinder, the Enneagram, and my cultural environment, I am impressed with how both assessments confirm certain core elements that make me who I am. Both affirm that I must be true to myself as well as the best version of myself. Both also affirm that I can easily live in the clouds, the future, or some idealized vision of the future.

Realizing who we are by self-reflecting about our strengths, weaknesses, and cultural values only goes so far. Though I can begin to realize who I am, this cannot be fully completed until I know who I am not.

Whenever I enter into a meaningful conversation with someone, I often find myself bringing up StrengthsFinder or the Enneagram. I will often tell them about it and get them to do the test as we're hanging out that day. As I have invited many of my friends into the road of self-discovery, I am continually blown away by how different they are from me.

As much as I can learn about myself in isolation and solitude, it isn't very effective in the real world. The real world has real people with all sorts of quirks and personalities. And so the better I am in seeing the differences between us and embracing them, the better I can be in working with and being in relationship with them.

Nobody I have met views and sees the world the way I do nor approaches it in exactly the same way. My temperament, attitude, personality, strengths, passions, weaknesses and emotional capacity are all different.

And the more we come to realizing our uniqueness as well as our differences, the more we can then find greater clarity in the person that we can be and the life we can live.

Summary

- Self-discovery and Self-awareness is a key to self-fulfillment. You can't have the life you were made for if you don't know who you are.

- StrengthsFinder and the Enneagram are two very helpful resources in taking the first step to self-knowledge.

- Culture plays a big part in our personalities and it's important to know that different cultures understand life very differently.

- It's really hard to know who you are in isolation.

- To know you are is to know who you aren't. Acknowledge the real differences between you and other people.

CHAPTER 7

Rely on Relationships

"If you want to go fast, go alone. If you want to go far, go together."

—African proverb

"It is impossible for a hockey player, or Bill Joy,
or Robert Oppenheimer, or any other outlier for that matter,
to look down from their lofty perch and say with truthfulness,
"I did this, all by myself." Superstar lawyers and math whizzes and
software entrepreneurs appear at first blush to lie outside ordinary
experience. But they don't. They are products of history
and community, of opportunity and legacy."

—Malcom Gladwell

As human beings, we were made to be in relationship.

As relational beings, we need people. We are all hurt and broken people
with a limp, needing a crutch. None of us can be content in complete

isolation. It's why for an inmate the worst punishment is solitary confinement. We go crazy if we aren't connected.

However, what I'm talking about is more than just a connection. More than just small talk over the water cooler. We need deep, meaningful relationships and conversations. But these relationships don't come naturally nor easily.

Relationships are freaking hard.

And given our Western value of independence and individualism, to rely on anything is hard. It challenges the fabric of our being. If we rely on someone, are we really who we are? Are we really that mature? That grown up?

We live in paradoxical times. Where romantic relationships are everything, but seemingly very few of us can find someone, we are willing to spend money on apps, services, and seminars to achieve this ideal relationship. Yet, we are, at the very same time, careless with the relationships we already do have. Family, work, even our own friends often get a back seat when it comes to the "important" things in life: career and romance.

As a person whose work has been primarily in the form of community development, I have learned, seen, and experienced the benefits of being in meaningful relationships. From my learnings and experiences, I have discovered that there are essentially five different relationship communities that we can have and that we need:

Parental: 1 on 1
Vulnerable: 1–3
Familial: 6–12
Purposeful: 20–100
Social: 100+

The Parental: the 1 on 1

Children need and rely on their parents. And as children, as people who are never perfect, we are always in need of parents. I am not referring solely to biological parents, however. Though they are certainly most needed and valued, we need even more. As the African proverb says, it takes a village to raise a child.

In order for us to properly grow, we need a village of parents, aunts, and uncles who will love and guide us. Whether we call them mentors or role-models, what we need are people we can look up to, respect, and listen to. People we can lean on, fall to, and learn from. In good times and bad.

We need someone who will affirm us. Who can affirm our strengths, acknowledge our limitations, and call us to be better and all that we can be.

We need guidance. We need someone to show us the way forward. To help us discern what is true, good, and beautiful in our lives and then live that out.

I am indebted to the many older and wiser people in my faith community who have invested in me. I would not be who or where I am today without them. I am also indebted to the older people whom I have paid, counselors and coaches, whose expertise in specific areas have enabled me to thrive.

The Vulnerable: 1–3

We need partners. Life is a journey, and it would be a terrible journey to go at it alone. Sure you have Gandalf, but he can't be there for you always. We need our Samwises. We need deep, intimate friendships; friends whom we trust and can be our true selves around.

Given our emotional capacity and time, most of us could probably only sustain a few at most. For the typical person, this would be a spouse and/or a best friend.

However, there are a few deep problems I have observed with finding these relationships. The problems rest in the very areas I indicated that help you know who you are and what to do with your life: passion, pain, power, and principles.

In our relationships, when we don't know our passion, pain, power, and principles, when we can't articulate and express them, it derails our ability to cultivate good and life-giving relationships.

Passion: We don't know how to love well. We don't know how to labor. To sacrifice. We all want to be in a romantic relationship, but the reality is that most of us are not willing to give up our preferences for another, let alone our life.

Pain: We are emotionally unhealthy. We overreact, blow things out of proportion, and take things too seriously and too personally. We become over-attached and needy. We are ashamed of our pain and hide it.

Power: We don't know our strengths and how to use them to bless others. We don't have anything to offer the relationships.

Principles: We don't share the same worldview. We don't agree on what is true, good, and beautiful in this world.

All of us want to be in a relationship, romantically or not, with someone who can love well, and who is in touch with their feelings and can express them and deal with them in a healthy way. Someone who doesn't simply take in the relationship, but who gives. And we want someone who can share our principles and priorities and truly walk with us in life.

BEING IS GREATER THAN DOING

The Familial: 6–12

We, as human beings, born of an intimate relationship, are the fruit of a family. We are the fruit of yes two people of an intimate and sexual relationship, but we are also the fruit of their parents, and most likely, aunts, uncles, brothers, sisters, and cousins.

The family unit is a universal and time-tested way of life. In a very insightful cultural commentary, Mike Breen reveals the pattern and progression of desire in Western culture when it comes to the family unit. In the 90s, we had Home Improvement. Tim Allen, his wife, their three kids, and Wilson. What did everyone want back in the day? The prototypical family unit.

Then at some point things changed. We stopped watching shows about a group of people that lived in the same house and were of the same blood, and instead, began watching a group of people who lived on the same floor and drank the same coffee. They navigated together through the hardships of divorce, being on a "break," and unemployment. But also the joys and laughs of relationships, children, and work.

We stopped wanting a family and started wanting friends.

Who can really say they don't want to just have a bunch of best/good friends that live on the same floor of their apartment building and journey together in the difficulties and joys of relationships, work, and life? That was the dream. It might even still be. *Seinfeld, Sex and the City, How I Met Your Mother*, and *New Girl* are but a few of the easiest examples I can think of that also point to the life that we want.

But then something else happened. Things shifted and the rise of the family unit came back. But it came back differently. Now, there's a grandfather. But he's married to a young and attractive Latina woman, raising her teenage son. There's an uncle, but he's gay, married, and has an Asian daughter. Then there's the "typical" husband and wife with three kids, but even they aren't that typical.

Modern family. Who doesn't want to be modern? To be a modern man or woman? And who doesn't want a modern family? A family that isn't simply this self-contained unit of a couple and their children, but one that is bigger and embraces the world.

We want friends that feel like family, but also a family that feels like friends. Kind of like how Ross and Monica were friends and yet also brother and sister at the same time.

How amazing would it be to have our family and friends integrated into the same community? Journeying together as a single unit through the frustrations and joys of life. Watching and walking alongside each other over years and seeing the full growth of one another.

We need Gandalf and Samwise, along with Merry, Pippin, Legolas and Gimli. The term "fellowship" comes from the Greek word *"koinonia."* *Koinonia* was used in Ancient Greek to refer to and describe a business partnership. When two people were in *koinonia* or fellowship together, they were not only friends, but partners, fellow sojourners towards a common goal and mission. We need a fellowship of something!

The Purposeful: 12–100

True community has always formed and happened when people of a common goal and mission cross paths and journey together. When soldiers fight together, they form a bond stronger than any common friendship formed back at home. Why? Because they are fighting together for a common and shared goal, mission, and purpose.

BEING IS GREATER THAN DOING

True community isn't simply a group of people who know each other, despite common and traditional belief. Real, deep community is much more and much better.

I love going to the gym. I'm not one who talks to a lot of people. I'm not a gym rat by any means. But I do appreciate the community. I love those moments when I walk in, and I see people of all ages, all working out for health, fitness, and aesthetics.

I love it when I actually recognize and know someone. There's Matthew, a 70+ year old man who likes to bench press and bicep curl with the barbell.

Gary, a 60+ year old man who knows everyone by name and who lovingly greets everyone as they enter.

Jason, who is a few years younger than me and is super jacked. He is the back king, and I aspire to one day have a back as thick as his.

Christina, who went to high school with me, but whom I never really talked to. She is a sports fanatic and is recovering from a very bad knee injury. Like really bad. Yet, she comes to the gym, squats, bench presses, and lifts despite her injury because she loves to and wants to become stronger and better.

Despite not really knowing any of these people personally well, I love being part of this community. We all have a common passion and goal. Getting healthy, jacked, and shredded.

We all need this type of community. A community of like-minded individuals that share a common set of principles and goals. This could be your gym, your company, your faith center, the PTA, or a sports league.

In a purposeful community, you don't need to completely fit in or have everyone love you to be involved and reap the benefits. Because you share and pursue a common love and purpose, the differences don't matter as much. I would never talk to Matthew or Christina in my regular life, but because of our passion for fitness, we can find a common ground and, therefore, a common bond.

We need people and communities in our lives like Elrond and the elves of Rivendell, Galadriel and the Wood Elves, the people of Rohan and Gondor!

The Social: +100

Lastly, we all need a social community.

Although the purposeful community is amazing, it does not completely fill your social needs. As much as I love going to the gym, I don't live at the gym, nor would I ever want to. I also don't want to spend all my time with Chandler, Ross, and Joey. Nor would I want to literally spend all my time with my wife and kids at home (if I ever have them).

I want to be part of something bigger. A network of relationships joined together by a common bond. I think of Belle in Beauty and the Beast as she walks down the road just living her life. Borrowing a book from the library, saying hi to the butcher, baker, and candlestick maker.

The times when people used to look each other in the eye and say hello to one another on the street are long gone, unfortunately. We neither look at people we encounter on the streets, nor do we say hello. It saddens me that this doesn't exist anymore and that a lot of people I know wouldn't even want it.

I think it's why I love coffee shops. In the coffee shop everyone is connected both geographically and experientially. We all live in the area or are all going to work, studying, or connecting with a friend. We also all need coffee. In Belle's village, it was simply surviving and living.

I love being a part of the Whole Foods community. One that is social, health, and beauty conscious. I don't know anyone there and no one knows me, yet I feel a bond between everyone there, however slight. We are connected by our appreciation for organic and healthy foods. We appreciate beautiful and aesthetically pleasing interior design. And we don't mind financially suffering a bit more for it.

I love being part of a faith community around the world. Wherever I go, I can find a place to worship along with other people who share my faith.

I love being part of the Chinese Canadian/American/Australian/not-born-in China or Hong Kong community. No matter where we grew up, we share a common childhood, culture and love for greasy dim sum.

As the cheesy and overplayed Jack Johnson song goes, we are better together. We feel better, get better, and do better with others.

We need a Middle-Earth. We need a kingdom. We need something after the war.

Summary

- There are five different types of relationships that we can all benefit from and are all necessary to complete flourishing. They are:

  - The Parental (1 on 1)

  - The Vulnerable (1-3)

  - The Familial (6–12)

  - The Purposeful (20-100)

  - The Social (100+)

CHAPTER 8

Reflect Regularly

> "Understanding is the first step to acceptance, and only with acceptance can there be recovery."
>
> **—JK Rowling**
>
> "Experience is not always the kindest of teachers, but it is surely the best."
>
> **—Spanish proverb**

In order to grow, we have to be self-aware.

In order to be self-aware, we need to reflect.

Socrates said the unexamined life is not worth living.

Self-awareness, self-examination, self-reflection is crucial, absolutely critical to being your best self. I assume that I don't have to convince you on this or else you wouldn't still be here.

If you aren't reflecting, you aren't growing; and if you aren't growing, then you are either just existing or potentially dying. Healthy things grow. Healthy things multiply and bear fruit. Plants, trees, animals, our bodies— when they're healthy, they grow and good things come from them.

Some people think of life as a school, a constant opportunity to learn and grow. However, like any form of education, if you don't engage and do the homework, you aren't gonna learn let alone pass. How do you get more than an A for participation in the school of life? You need to reflect. Spending the time to actually think about what you've heard, seen, and experienced and ask good questions.

How does reflection happen though? How do we purposefully reflect amidst the infinite amount of time we could spend and the many options of how?

Because you, and the world, are constantly changing, in order to keep up, you must reflect just as often or as quickly. This requires you to not just stop once in a while and ask yourself if this is still what you want to do and should do; it requires you to do it regularly and rigorously.

In my opinion, you, at the very least, need to intentionally reflect every day, each week, and every season. How you do that is flexible and will be explored further in a moment.

Daily

A common way to reflect is to simply wake up or go to bed a bit earlier and ask yourself when in the last 24 hours you felt most alive and when you felt most dead. The regular practice of asking these two questions will reveal a lot about the state of your soul and cause you to see the dissonance of your life.

I try to practice this as often as I can. In doing so, I have realized that I often feel alive when I connect meaningfully to other people and help them be their best. Though this certainly has been pointed out through various relationships and tests, there is another level of affirmation that only comes through the regular reflection.

And I have observed I am most dead when I feel disconnected in my relationships; when I get into a fight or get a sense that I've upset or hurt someone I care about; and when I didn't have a chance that day to express my strengths in pursuit of my passions.

This daily reflection could take as short as a couple minutes or as long to 10–20, depending on how familiar you are with this practice and how deeply you want to reflect on it.

Weekly

Unfortunately, life isn't that simple where we only need to reflect a couple minutes a day. Often something happens each week that rattles our lives. Maybe it's a fight with a friend or an amazing date. Maybe it's a book you read or a TED talk you watched. When these larger and more impactful events happen, we need more time to reflect. The bigger the event the more time we need.

The challenge is not in the recognition that we need more time to reflect upon bigger events (good and bad), but creating the space for it. Reflecting over our day for a couple of minutes doesn't take a lot of effort. Most of us, however, are living quite full and busy lives and would probably find it difficult to set aside and spend 30–60 minutes to simply think, meditate, and journal.

If you don't craft out time intentionally each week to stop and reflect, you will most likely naturally just go on living life with event after event happening without ever asking how that made you feel, why it happened, and how you should respond. Though this may seem like a luxury to the lucky few, you have to recognize how much is at stake.

Life is just too complicated and too much of a gong show at times for you not to.

Seasonally

Now I might just be beating the proverbial dead horse, but let me say it again: life is complicated. So much crap happens that you can't control, and yet you are also ultimately responsible for the life that you live.

This truth of life is both comforting and terrifying. It's why we may require long bouts of time of intense reflection. This is generally known as a "sabbatical"; the intentional act of removing oneself from their work to rest, to reflect and come back ready to kill it.

The word "sabbatical" comes from the Hebrew word Sabbath, which means rest. In the Jewish scriptures, God told the Jewish people to rest once a week. This was, however, not just a day off, but rather an intentional 24-hour period spent resting and connecting to God and to their family/community.

According to Jewish tradition and belief, this "command" to rest (one of the 10 commandments: thou shall take a break; thou shall take a Kit Kat) was given to them at a time when they were slaves to the Egyptians. It's really important for our conversation that we understand the meaning of sabbatical so bear with me.

BEING IS GREATER THAN DOING

The Jews were slaves to Egypt for 500 years. Egypt did not have human rights or governments or agencies that protected people. Slavery was alright. It was A OK. Abe Lincoln and Will Wilberforce would not exist until thousands of years later. But at some point in time, this guy named Moses came and rescued the Jews from Egyptian captivity.

And once they had a moment to breathe and begin their journey to finding a piece of land that they could settle in and call home, God tells them to rest once a week.

"You want me to do what?"

"What is this rest you talk about?"

Rest is counterintuitive to many cultures it seems.

Sabbath means rest. But instead of a weekly rest, we use sabbatical as a season of rest from work usually. Taking a sabbatical doesn't only have to be done in the context of work, however.

For decades in hopes of gaining a greater clarity for their future, young people all over the country have been taking a summer or year off to travel, explore, work, volunteer, or anything that expands their minds about life. Taken unintelligently, unintentionally, and unreflectively this is just a vacation and our grandparents were right that we are just wasting our money and having fun.

But when done intelligently, intentionally, and reflectively, a sabbath can be amazing for any major decision. Should I take this new job? How will it affect my life and family? Should I move for that new job? Should I ask her to marry me? Should I end this relationship before he asks me to marry him? Or simply, what am I doing with my life?

The word humility comes from the word "humus" which means "from the ground. We are people of the ground and humility comes from remembering that. We cannot, no matter who we think we are, solve all our problems head on.

For myself, I once spent a Friday evening and the entire day Saturday without any food or technology in the spare room of my grandparents' basement to make a decision that I thought was important: should I ask my ex-girlfriend to take me back. We had broken-up five months ago, and we were pretty serious when we were going out. If I were to ask her to take me back, I had better be sure. I had better be sure I actually wanted it, could do it, and see a future with her.

After this time of fasting and reflection, I decided I could with some confidence ask her to take me back. However, she said no. There may not be a more painful time in my entire life than the following days, weeks, and months after. But looking back, I don't regret any of it. I think I did it reflectively, responsibly, and respectfully. I'm not proud with most of the times I've approached romance, but this is one in which I am.

Our reflection doesn't need to produce "results" for it to be productive.

She and I are now friends. We worked together on the same team for a little while. And for a season on Tuesday afternoons, we would get together with other coworkers, put on an exercise video on YouTube, and work out.

So that's basically why we should reflect and when. But we haven't yet discussed how.

Individually and relationally.

There are essentially two ways in which we can approach reflection: individually and relationally.

Individually

Meditation: Being silent and still, allowing your mind to let go of all the worries of the future and being present to any thoughts or revelations that may come.

Reading: Reading something serious that would force your brain to slow down and think about life.

Journaling: Writing down everything and anything that comes to mind. As you force yourself to write your thoughts and feelings, your brain is forced to slow down, providing you with a clearer head and a greater ability to reflect.

Worldview Reflection: Asking good questions to yourself like "What should the world be like and what is my role?" "What is true, good, and beautiful?" and "Am I headed in the right direction?"

Any of these ways to self-reflect can be a helpful tool in thinking clearly and wisely about life, though we may prefer one over the others. The most important aspect of reflection is simply moving oneself from distraction and slowing down. If you can ignore the distractions of this world and your life and be quiet enough to be in tune with your soul, you will always hear something.

If those sound too difficult for you, just get rid of your phone for as long as possible. You will naturally begin to reflect and think more deeply as you become more connected to your surroundings and self. This unfortunately, might also be the most difficult. Our devices are making us in many ways dumber and less self-aware. I don't think you need to be convinced of this. Sherry Turkle's *Reclaiming Conversation: The Power of Talk in a Digital Age* is a stimulating and prophetic word into our current and changing culture. I highly recommend reading it. Whether we are consciously aware of it or not, our phones prevent us from reflection and thus growth, self-development, and life.

Relationally

We can't do it alone, which I have iterated and won't reiterate. However, I want to emphasize that as much as we need people and communities in their various sizes, intimacy levels, and beauties to encourage, support us, and simply make life worth living, we also need them to challenge us.

We need our various relationship communities to call us out, call us up, and call us forward.

None of us have complete 20/20 vision on our lives and the world. None of us are perfect; therefore, we cannot see or know everything,

You and I, I hate to say it, are not as smart, emotionally-mature, and self-aware as we think we are. This is almost fundamentally against the grain of what our culture of individualism and independence tell us, but if you are reading this book, you are open to the idea, to whatever degree, that we need other people to speak into our lives.

We certainly need people to encourage us, to call us forward in life, and affirm our strengths and qualities. To simply be there for us.

But we also need people in our life to lovingly challenge and confront us. To straight up tell us we're being dumb or crazy.

None of us are perfect. In fact, we are far from it. We're selfish, self-absorbed, and self-unaware despite our best efforts. We could be doing something out of the best intentions but could be completely off the mark.

There have been and presently are "leaders," people of power and position who may have done things differently if they had a close group of friends, a mentor, or a parent in their life that just said, "What the heck? Are you serious? You want to what? Tell me you're joking."

Chances are you are not a world leader or someone about to make a decision that will affect the lives of thousands, if not millions. But we are all making plans and doing things we think are right and that affect others. What makes us any different than those delusional world leaders aside from the magnitude of the consequences of our actions?

How do you reflect well then in relationship? First, you need to humble yourself and recognize who you are. You need to remember you are from the earth and recognize you are not perfect.

You then need to give permission to close ones you love and respect, and who love and respect you, to say the things you might not necessarily want to, but need to hear.

I have a close group of two guy friends, whom I could not live without. I am confident I would certainly be less alive and a lot deader inside without them. At one point in my life, I was in a relationship I knew I shouldn't have been in.

When this girl and I initially started getting to know one another, it was harmless. We were just two people getting to know each other. However, it quickly snowballed into an emotional roller-coaster that not only harmed myself but her as well. At a point of desperation and vulnerability, I told my friends in our group chat about how I had been struggling to end this relationship because of how unhealthy it was for me and for her.

Given how much I prided myself on having a good control over my life, I told them I was too emotional and ashamed of myself for even being in this situation, and so I asked them to simply pray for me.

One of my friends wouldn't accept that. He sternly, but lovingly said, "Hey Ryan, I know you don't want to talk about this, but I think we should. I think we should get together and meet up tonight. To talk and to pray. Would you be open to this?"

"Did I not just say that I didn't want to talk about it let alone meet about it?"

But because I trusted in my friends, I agreed despite every part of me that didn't want to.

There are moments in our life when we know we are truly loved, no matter what we've done or how badly we've screwed up.

That night was one of those moments.

I didn't feel judged or condemned. I felt challenged, encouraged, and most of all, loved. I am truly blessed to not just have people in my life that love me and are willing to challenge me, but also to have people that know how to. My relationship with the girl ended that night, and I could not have been more grateful to have had such friends like I did in my life.

It's not easy to love a person truthfully. The truth isn't always pleasant, but it's the truth. And love is certainly not easy. It requires patience and kindness (two qualities that I have very little of). But this type of love is critical to our well-being. To our personal development and flourishing.

If I may use the analogy of us as a plant, be it a flower or a tree, sometimes we need to be pruned. We need someone else to do the hard task of pointing out the unnecessary and harmful parts growing in our life and calling us to cut them out. The question is, will we do it? Will we individually reflect on the reflection of our trusted relationships and act? We are all addicts to something, and we at times all need an intervention. But more on that in the next chapter.

To reflect relationally, we need to have trusted relationships with people that will genuinely listen to us, and who will speak into our lives with truth and grace. It could be as big as an A.A. meeting or as small as a mentor or coach. How we reflect relationally is by being in deep relationship with other people.

Remember and Remind

In our overloaded age of information, thoughts, and ideas, it's so easy to lose our way. To forget and slowly lose our grasp on the principles that began our journey. In addition to regular reflection, we also need regular reminders. As often as we reflect, we should also remember.

For every minute we spend reflecting on our life, maybe we should spend the same amount of time reminding ourselves what life is all about. Reflecting is the proactive act of thinking about what has and what will happen. Reminding is the proactive act of thinking of what is: what is true, what is good, and what is beautiful.

For people of traditional faith and spiritual traditions, this means regular reading and reflection of their scriptures both individually and communally.

We can learn from this universal and ancient tradition by regularly reading and reflecting on our own source of truth.

We all have a framework, a set of beliefs, about the world and the purpose of human life and our own life. And we need to be reminded of that. We all need a system to remind ourselves of what is true, good, and beautiful in this world. Whether that is hanging on to the fridge your family values, or having your life's creed as the wallpaper on your phone and computer, have your principles close.

I try to watch *The Matrix* at least once a year to remind me of some of my principles to the meaning of life. I also try to listen to specific love songs from the 90s which help to remind me what love is about (e.g. *Flying Without Wings* by Westlife).

Whatever it is, we are a forgetful and easily swayed people that need to be regularly reminded of the important things in life. To be reminded and then encouraged to live it out today, tomorrow and forever!

Summary

- Reflection must be regularly done to be done well.

- Reflection can be done daily, weekly, and seasonally.

- Different types of reflection require different amounts of time.

- Reflection can and should be done alone and with others.

- Purely reflecting isn't helpful or fruitful unless you remember and remind yourself of your truth and values. Your principles.

CHAPTER 9

Rule Your Life

"Following your heart is easy, following your brain is tough."

—Gregory House M.D.

"Sow a thought, reap an action; sow an action, reap a habit; sow a habit, reap a character; sow a character, reap a destiny."

—Unknown

Just thinking about life, let alone actually living it, stresses me out.

Like, I think:

Is this what I am going to be doing for the rest of my life?
Will I ever meet someone that will sweep me off my feet?
Will I ever be comfortable in my own skin?
Am I going to make any difference in the world?

One of my central beliefs about life, highlighted throughout this book, is that we have control over our lives, the direction of it, and are able to respond to the setting and events we find ourselves in. We might not have perfect control over ourselves and everything around us, but that doesn't mean we are helpless and privy to every wave and gust of wind.

If we, if you and I, really want to be our best possible selves and live the life we were born for, then we're going to need to actually do something about it.

Good things, great things, the best things rarely, if ever, happen by accident. Yet most of us live as if life is a lottery, and we're all just waiting to see if we hit the jackpot.

If pursuing our passion is a function of our labor, how much more labor then is required in becoming our very best?

In the very true and wise words of Brittany, "You gotta work b****. Now get to work!"

Nothing worthy in life comes easy. Not even love.

It requires blood, sweat, and tears.

Persistence, patience, and sacrifice.

Dedication, strategy, and a team.

Have you ever met a successful entrepreneur? Successful entrepreneurs are almost impossible to not respect in some way.

Whether it came naturally or they learned it, entrepreneurs know the fundamentals of work and life. They know that all good things come at a cost, and they hustle their butt off for it. They also know they aren't super humans so they need other people to help them.

Whether it's fake or not, they know they have to be nice, network, and get people to buy into the vision and business. Entrepreneurs will sacrifice everything in order to pursue and reach their goal. They move back home, they clear out their bank account, and wake up every day at 6 am and start working at Starbucks at 7.

Entrepreneurs are hard not to respect from a performance perspective. Putting aside their character flaws, which we all have, it's hard to look at their work ethic and all that they have risked and achieved and not tip our hats off to them.

If you want to be your best self and live your best life, you need to act like an entrepreneur because well, you are. You are the boss of your life. The one solely responsible for leading and ensuring its success.

Life is not just going to happen. It's not going to fall or be placed in your lap, and no one is going to help you without expecting something in return.

These are the hard realities of business and of life.

But this doesn't mean that life needs to be a soul-suffocating grind, though.

I am indebted to my colleague, Ken Shigematsu, for emphasizing and sharing the concept of a "rule of life." In essence, a rule of life is a framework in which we live each of our days. He explains that although the word "rule" is usually frowned upon and received with almost entirely negative feelings, it's a good and necessary component to any good life and to any form of flourishing.

You see, the word "rule" comes from the Latin word meaning "trellis." A trellis, for those who are unfamiliar with the ways of agriculture, is a wooden structure used to support the physical growth of a plant. You know, the ones used to support grapevines.

Think of the production of wine: Wine comes from grape juice. Grape juice comes from grapes. Grapes grow on vines. If you want more sales, more money, you're going to need more wine; you're going to need more grapes.

You're going to need more vines.

Vines are hard to grow though. They usually grow along walls and trees. If someone wanted to produce a ton of wine and, therefore, grapevines, they're going to need a lot of something to support the growth. Vines are thin, but they, for whatever reason, produce these heavy balls we call grapes. If the vines grow too many or too big of grapes, the vines will fall down. Nobody likes to fall down, and neither do plants.

As a result, farmers long ago cultivated a simple practice of growing grape vines and other plants next to a wood structure that looks kind of like a triangular fence where the vine attaches itself to it and grows without limits.

It may be confined to the trellis, but it can grow way more and produce way more grapes and larger grapes than without it.

We require a life trellis. We require a "rule," a creed, or manifesto that we adhere to and hold to for the sake of our growth and flourishing.

Sure we may be "tied" down. "Confined." But would you rather be confined to your own self-determined rules and flourish in them or would you rather be "free" and unconstrained, grasping for any wall or form of stability?

I am convinced of this in part because of Donald Miller who said, "We don't understand personal growth because we don't understand agricultural growth." To add onto Miller, I would argue that we also don't understand personal growth because we don't understand engineering.

In either case, we don't understand how anything grows or is built. No matter what analogy we use for life, none of us seem to be taking it seriously.

If we were to compare ourselves to a plant, we don't water ourselves or expose ourselves to the light every day nor do we plant ourselves in good soil.

If we compare ourselves to a home, we don't have a foundation. We haven't done the hard work of digging deep into ourselves, gutting all the crap out, and building a firm framework.

From John Maxwell to Jim Collins, leadership and business authors often refer to a famous race between two teams in Antarctica. Both teams were well-prepared, equipped, and ready to lead. One team, however, decided to go at a certain pace every day whereas the other team decided to go as far as they could on good weather, and hide out in bad weather.

The first team won.

Why? Because according to Collins, they implemented what he now calls a "20-Mile March." Basically, people who progress and succeed are the ones who work and take steps forward regardless of their circumstances. Though it may make sense to run as fast as we can when we're feeling good and Netflix when we're feeling alright, we can't predict or control our circumstances and mood and, therefore, will fall behind those who make progress every day.

When it comes to becoming your best self, you have to recognize how you best grow and then make the rules to foster it. If you were always told to wake up early in the morning to exercise but have never been able to wake up, you probably won't ever wake up early to go to the gym.

Instead, you might prefer to go after work or after dinner. If that is the case, you are going to then need to schedule your days and weeks to create time to work out before or after dinner. There needs to be rules or else we will go when we want, and how often do any of us want to go to the gym? It's too cold in the winter, and it's too nice in the summer. It's so easy to make excuses to not work out.

We need to say "no" to good things in order to say "yes" to great things. Yes, it might be fun to go out for drinks or dinner with your coworkers after work. But if you make this a habit and a bigger priority than going to the gym, then you aren't going to progress in your fitness goals.

If you don't make it a rule to go out once a week or however often, fun times complaining about the boss after work with a couple of beers will be impossible to decline.

If chapter 4 was about our major priorities in life, then this chapter is about the everyday rules we make in order to live out our priorities.

Guard Your Hands (Time and Energy)

My friend, John, one time wanted to hang out with an old acquaintance of ours, Billy. Billy has run into John and me hanging out a couple of times throughout the years and has always suggested the three of us should hang out next time.

Due to life schedules, the only available time for us to get together would be Saturday noon for lunch. Because I work Sunday to Thursday, Saturdays are a very precious day for me. It's one of my "weekend" days, but it's also the only day I can see and spend time with my friends as all of them work on Fridays.

I have a rule that I only do things that give me life on Saturday. There's a lot of things I don't want to do throughout the week. They're usually good things. Necessary things. But not things I jump out of bed excited for.

Life has obligations and duties that we can't always say no to, nor should we. But I've made it a rule to be as ruthlessly selfish as possible with my Saturdays. So when John asked if I wanted to hang out with Billy, I just said no.

"No thanks," I told him.

"When would a good time be for you?"

"Never . . . It's not that I have anything against the guy. Billy's awesome. It's just that there is always going to be a Billy wanting to grab a bite or drink and have some small talk. It's not as if Billy really wants to see me anyway. He doesn't really want to know how I'm doing or get into anything deep. He just wants to talk about the old days and crack some jokes. If you want to go hang out with him, then go ask him and hang out with him. You don't need me."

"Ouch. That's cold, dude."

Maybe it is. I'm not Mother Teresa though. I have not dedicated my entire life and all of my resources to every person in the world. I would like to think I've dedicated my entire life and all of its resources to something beyond my own wants and needs, but that doesn't need to include every person. Anyway, Billy doesn't *really* care about me or my life and it's not like I am that great of a conversationalist either. If I knew Billy was hurting or lonely maybe I'd be more open but I'm pretty sure he's doing alright without me.

Who knows what would have happened at that lunch? Actually I do know because it happens to me all the time. I do something I don't want to do, spend money I don't want to spend, and have a conversation I don't need to have. What happens? I get frustrated, tired, and drained. I didn't receive any life from the conversation, and the people that I love and connect with later are going to have to pay for it. I won't have the necessary energy for them. The extrovert in me may be tapped out, and I won't be able to give the needed love and attention that they need.

I'm not perfect, and I can't be all things to all people. I just don't have the energy or time for it.

In order to be your best self and live your best life, you have to be ruthlessly ruled. You have to be ruthless with keeping first things first and protecting yourself so you can live out your principles and priorities.

Your time is an expendable and limited resource. We are always and constantly "busy."

"How are you?"

"Busy!"

"That's . . . not what I asked you."

We wear busyness as a badge of honor. The busier we are, regardless of how much of that is wasted time, the prouder we feel, as if being a rested and structured person is a bad thing. Somehow not having control of our lives and bouncing from one obligation to another is a good and desirable thing.

If we want to be better people, if we want to be our best and live our best, we have to be people of rules. We will need to protect our time and energy.

We will also need to protect our emotions.

Guard your Heart (Emotions)

There is a resource, however, that is exhaustive and much more complicated than our time or energy, so I'm giving it a category of its own: emotions.

"Guard your heart, for it is the wellspring of life," says the Jewish scriptures.

Our hearts are arguably that which controls our entire being. Sure our bodies are controlled neurologically by our brains. But our brains are subject to our hearts. Our passion, our desires, our wills.

The heart knows what it wants and nothing the brain tells it can convince it otherwise. Just try convincing someone in an unhealthy relationship—where everyone, including them, know they shouldn't be in it—to get out of it. Good luck there.

Because our emotions are so strong and so important it's impossible to overemphasize this.

When we are overly emotional, we say and do things we normally wouldn't do, for better and for worse. It can cause us to do beautiful romantic gestures. But it can also make us act like complete psychopaths (having often acted like one myself).

People who are and live out their best self are emotionally healthy people.

They know when to say yes, and more importantly when to say no. They aren't controlled by the opinions of others and are not trying to prove themselves to someone and even themselves.

Emotionally healthy people have healthy boundaries.

They say no to and distance themselves from unhealthy people not because they're jerks or because they don't have a heart, but because they know they aren't perfect, that they're not God, and they have more than just that one person to worry about in their life.

They think "OKAY this person is needy. Super needy. And as much as I would like to help, this person doesn't seem to want help or is unwilling to change. There are a lot of needs in the world, Bob, Sue, and Steven are all going through things right now. If I keep saying yes to David, I'm not going to have the time nor emotional capacity for Bob, Sue, and Steven. David is going to drain me so much that I'm just going to want to veg out on Netflix at home."

In the Bible, there is a story about a farmer with a bunch of seeds. As he was going for a walk one day, he threw the seeds onto four different pieces of land. It says:

"As he was scattering the seed, some fell along the path, and the birds came and ate it up. Some fell on rocky places, where it did not have much soil. It sprang up quickly, because the soil was shallow. But when the sun came up, the plants were scorched, and they withered because they had no root. Other seed fell among thorns, which grew up and choked the plants. Still other seed fell on good soil, where it produced a crop—a hundred, sixty or thirty times what was sown."—Matthew 13:4–8

Moral of the story? Your environment matters. The people you surround yourself and choose to interact with matter. Your work matters. Everything matters because everything takes up your time and energy, and influences your emotions.

When you put yourself in bad environments, you either get eaten up, burnt out, or choked. But when you put yourself in good environments, you can bring exponentially more value in the world.

Summary

- Rules are good.

- Rules set you up for your success and your defense.

- A Rule of Life is a set of rules or principles to live by.

CHAPTER 10

Reinvest In and Raise Up Others

> "If you think you are too small to make a difference
> you have never spent a night with a mosquito."
>
> —African proverb

> "I am indebted to my father for living,
> but to my teacher for living well."
>
> —Alexander the Great

It's said that those who can't do, teach.

Although I'm sure my high school English teacher probably would rather have been a successful author, for the most part, I don't think this statement is true.

In reality, teaching and doing are two very different activities that require two completely different sets of skills. I would even argue that teaching is way more difficult since none of us seem to really know all that much about anything.

Teaching is a natural component of human living. Whether it's in the classroom, the office, or before we tuck our kids into bed, we are born to be communicators and teachers. Teaching is just a part of life, and it's something we all love to do.

Why else would people be constantly telling me something or giving me advice when I never asked them to?

Teaching is also how we learn. In high school, a few teachers required us to teach the class about our project as part of the project grade. At the time, I thought they were just being lazy and using it as an excuse to take up a few more classes. Even if this were their true intention, it doesn't change the fact that preparing for my presentation is when I really learned and owned my material. Not when I Wikipedia'd everything.

Teaching both fulfills our human instinct to pass on knowledge and influence others and also our human desire to grow and learn.

Teaching is one of the most effective activities in human flourishing. We simultaneously give and receive. It's where we make a difference and where we are made different.

You and I are the product and fruit of the love and labor of others physically as well as intellectually. Others have been teaching us. Every helping hand we've been given, every book we've read, and every idea we've heard has been an investment into our lives, whether we implemented it or not.

Learning is so crucial to developing ourselves, but we also need to give back and teach others.

BEING IS GREATER THAN DOING

As the CEO, CFO, and COO of our lives, we are both responsible for the profits (our happiness) and also the "employees" who work for us. Though no one technically works for us, the people in our lives do play a role somehow in serving and aiding us in achieving our happiness. What kind of boss would we be if we did not reciprocate and ensure they also grew and flourished?

It is just good business to develop leadership and skills in house and build off the relationships and loyalty that has developed over the years. You can only grow the company as far as the capacity of your employees. And although you can fire and hire to find the right people, turnover is still very costly.

In the same way, if we continually bounce from relationship to relationship, never staying in any meaningful relationship for too long, we lose something in the turnover. We lose the resources we spend in acquiring and building new friendships, but we also lose the hidden and growing potential in those we are already in a relationship with.

To truly be your best and to be a good boss, you have to give back. You have to reinvest what you've been given back to others.

You are response-able then to use all that you've become and all that you've attained to help others become who they are meant to be. There would be nothing short of a cultural, intellectual, and moral revolution in the world if we all took this one requirement seriously.

What I am suggesting, practically speaking, is that we must become parents and teachers to someone else. Not birth parents but life parents. Not school teachers necessarily but life teachers. Just as we need mentors and coaches in our lives, those one on one relationships, so do others. People need you. People need you to reinvest what you've been given into them.

Why can't we, why can't you and I, reinvest what we've been given into others? Surely there cannot be a negative outcome to this. We are starved for mentors and for relationships. Someone who cares about us and others and is willing to freely sacrifice something for our flourishing. Someone who will dream and push us beyond what we can envision for ourselves in this moment.

Many people don't have enough mentors and positive relationships. We need to change that. We need to be better. We need to do better.

Surely if we did that, if we freely sacrificed for the flourishing of another human being, nothing but truth, goodness, and beauty would come out of it.

But how do we do that? That is probably the question that may be most relevant. How do I find people and begin reinvesting and teaching them? It's not like they're knocking on my door or posting it on craigslist.

1) Start with Who.

Simon Sinek, often referred to in many leadership talks, has one of the most popular Ted Talk videos ever. His book *Start with Why* is often mentioned as a must read. Sinek's basic premise and principle is that when we lead others, whether individually or organizationally, we must start with "why." We must start with the reason, the values, the principles in which we are being guided by rather than the end result. To quote Sinek, "Martin Luther King Jr had a dream, not a plan."

As much as I appreciate Sinek's contribution to the leadership community, I believe he misses something. He misses the "who." "Who am I and what do I have to offer?"

Anyone can offer a dream. Who doesn't have dreams? I'm sure all of us have someone we want to help, someone we want to add value to.

But before you begin to think about changing the world or another person's life, before you think about "why," you have to think about you.

How many people have ever offered you unsolicited advice for your life? People who have no authority, no experience, no position to be providing "insight" or "wisdom" in an area in which they have none? How frustrated did that make you? I bet pretty frustrated.

So why be that person to someone else?

When you start with you, when you first focus on seeking wisdom and experience, you will then become an ideal candidate to reinvest and raise up others.

That's pretty much the premise and basis of this entire book. The only thing you can change is yourself. If you want to see change, then you must be the change.

2) Do It Tactfully, Intentionally and Patiently (T.I.P.)

In our era of instant, where everything must happen now, we have become the least patient of people to say the least. If I have to wait more than three seconds for the website to load, I'm going to click refresh or close down the window all together. I hear that Korea has the fastest internet in the world and also the least patience when it comes to browser-loading speeds.

This lack of patience has bled into the way we help others. We want to help, but we want it to happen quickly and with as very little sacrifice as possible (and ideally none).

When we think about helping people, often we simplify the problem and provide a solution. This has proved ineffective and resulted in arguably negative outcomes for relief efforts worldwide. Although there have certainly been many lives saved and helped, it has not been without a cost.

Communities become dependent on Western aid and have lost the value of hard work and their creative ingenuity in business/economic development. We think if we just give enough money, at some point these people will hit equilibrium and will begin to self-develop and self-improve. To my knowledge so far, I don't know of any community in the world whose problems have been solved solely by monetary aid.

Likewise when we think about helping someone closer to home, we may not think the solution is a quick dime, but we still think it can be a quick something. A quick conversation or a quick word. If we just tell this person the truth, then all will be good. And if it isn't, it's their choice and their fault.

Too bad people here are no more different and no more complicated than the communities overseas.

Our friends, our family members, you and every human being on this planet needs more than just a hand out. It could come from a really great place, the greatest and most loving of intentions, but just as any child can attest, just because their parents have good intentions and all the love in the world, it doesn't mean it was helpful. By experience, we could probably agree it often had the exact opposite effect.

If we truly want to help others, to reinvest the great insights and learnings of our lives into others, we have to do it tactfully, intentionally, and patiently. That's my TIP for you.

Tactfully.
Intentionally.
Patiently.

And by no means am I an expert in this. I often lose patience and say it how it is "This is stupid. You're being crazy." And what I have learned time and time again from each of these mess-ups is that a bit more tact, intention, and patience never hurt anyone.

As I heard Donald Miller once say in regards to personal growth, "we have to think about it more as marinating than microwaving."

When you tell someone to read a book because you think it would be helpful, don't just tell her, show her. Buy the book for her. Lend her your own. Offer or even suggest to get together in a couple weeks to discuss what she's read so far and how it might apply to her life.

If you honestly think that book may be an answer to her problems, the salvation to her sad and miserable life, then treat that book as if it actually were and do everything you can to help her read, reflect, and respond to it.

If you want to get real ninja-like, start a book club of that book with a bunch of your friends and invite that particular friend into it so she doesn't feel so pressured, pathetic, or pitied.

Too often we send people with the best of intentions to counsellors, communities, and programs without doing the hard work of going with them. Rich parents send their kids to boarding schools or counsellors without ever doing the hard and real work of listening. At least that's what I see on TV.

3) Do it in Community

Change or growth, however, is not an easy thing. And it's rarely, if ever in the entire history of humanity, done by a single person. As much as we need to rely on others to encourage and support us in our own growth, we equally need a relationship-community to encourage and support us in the growth of others.

The only thing better than being part of a purposeful community (a group of like-minded and goal-oriented people) is being part of a group of people, a family, whose goal involves supporting, encouraging, and helping you help others. We all need a group of people, a partner at the very least who can walk with us as we walk with another.

We can't raise up others effectively if we can't rely on others humbly.

4) Do It in Love

When we think of an investment, any type, we always want the greatest return right? However much we put in, we would always be happier with 10x our investment than 2x. Because people are people and not a stock option or a piece of real-estate, when reinvesting in and raising up another, we must remember to do it in love and that love is not transactional.

The foundation of our reinvestment and raising up of another must be founded in love and not pragmatism. Trust me, I learned this the hard way.

I like things fast and efficient as much as anyone. I also like results. Something I've learned over time though is that when seeking the change of another person, we can't set an agenda or a time frame. Life just doesn't work like that.

BEING IS GREATER THAN DOING

When you raise a child, you hope it will be bumpless, that there will be no bad boyfriends, parties, or negative external influences on your child. Unfortunately, that is not the world we live in. All boys are bad and, therefore, all boyfriends will be too.

Parenting is hard work. Arguably the hardest work in the world. You don't get a break or a vacation, you don't get paid for it, you're rarely thanked for it, and you're committed for at least 18 years if not for life.

It's going to take a lot more than just the desire to have a child to keep a person in it. It's going to take more than just "responsibility" for the father to stay. It's going to need real and deep love.

And the same goes for when we wish to reinvest and raise up another for the long haul. Lots, and lots of love. Love, as Mandy Moore so famously made it, is . . .

"patient, love is kind. It does not envy, it does not boast, it is not proud. It does not dishonor others, it is not self-seeking, it is not easily angered, it keeps no record of wrongs. Love does not delight in evil but rejoices with the truth. It always protects, always trusts, always hopes, always perseveres."

Shoot son, that's a lot to ask of someone.

It's probably why none of us are being invested into or investing in others.

Just this week I watched the "new" Adam Sandler movie, *Sandy Wexler,* with Jennifer Hudson. In it Sandler plays a geeky, completely incompetent but deeply loving talent manager and Hudson plays the up and coming talent. (If you haven't seen it and care about knowing the end, I would suggest then to skip this part).

As the movie progresses, Hudson becomes bigger and bigger and eventually outgrows Sandler. Sandler, in loving humility, bows out and steps down from his role as her manager. As the story progresses, Hudson, still adjusting to the life of stardom, finds herself in unhealthy relationship after unhealthy relationship. It isn't until the very end that Sandler finally confesses his true feelings and love for her and Hudson reciprocates.

The most touching moment of the entire movie was at the very end where 20 years after they were married, they celebrate their anniversary with all of their friends. The movie ends with interview after interview of people whose lives had been touched and changed by Sandler, the loving and eventually competent talent manager.

This story along with almost any other story, regardless of genre, shows me that we have a need, a deep desire, to raise another up and to be raised up. Not just in the child-parent context, but in the human-human context. There is something fundamentally good and beautiful about parenting whether or not it is in the biological context.

None of us want to stay stagnant. None of us do not want to grow. And none of us want to do it alone.

To reinvest in and raise up another is not simply a requirement to true growth and maturity, but part of what it fundamentally means to be human. When we ignore or deny our desire to raise up another person, we deny our humanity. The good news is that this person is not limited or segregated to a biological child. Sure it may be the most natural and easiest way to have influence over another human being, but it is certainly not the only way.

Why do people become teachers and mentors? What is it about the stories of Sandy Wexler, Gandalf the Grey, Aladdin and the Genie, Simba and Pride Rock, Professor Xavier and the X-men that move our hearts? What is it about being invested in and investing in another that stirs our souls? That makes us scream, "I want and need to be a part of something like that."

It is our very human need to be parents.

BEING IS GREATER THAN DOING

To have influence and significance.

To make pure and good value.

However, a word of caution: just as much as it starts with you it also starts with them.

If I have learned anything from the *Walking Dead* and any other apocalyptic narrative is that we can't save those who don't want to be saved. We can't help those who don't want to be helped.

At a certain point, we have to recognize that the people we care about may not be willing nor want to change.

Unless the person you are trying to help is your child or your spouse who you have made a vow to love in sickness and in health (physically, mentally, emotionally and spiritually), there is a point where you have to accept the reality that this person isn't ready. That doesn't mean you give up entirely on the person forever. But it may mean that you re-evaluate and refocus your time and energy on other people and other things for the sake of your own well-being and as well as the world.

For those in an unhealthy relationship, something only you and those whom you trust and love can determine, it may mean ending the relationship. You're not married; you didn't make any vows before your community or your God saying you would stick it out. That's the whole point of dating: to figure out if you can and want to.

There is absolutely no shame in putting your own needs, your own mental, spiritual and emotional health first. And if your physical health even needs to be considered, I can emphatically and without hesitation say you need to get out of this.

We are made to be teachers, not saviors.

Summary

- We were made to teach. We were born to help others grow.

- Before we can help others, we need to be able to have a certain level of credibility.

- Being tactful, intentional, and patient with people is never a bad idea.

- We aren't God. We can't help people alone. We need others, a community, to truly help another flourish.

- Helping people is done best when you actually care about and love the person.

- Some people just don't want to change or want your help.

CHAPTER 11

Resist the Brokenness
and Replace with Beauty

> **"Our life is what our thoughts make it."**
>
> **—Marcus Aurelius**
>
> **"Good thoughts bear good fruit, bad thoughts bear bad fruit."**
>
> **—James Allen**

If there's anything that I've learned in my attempt and journey towards becoming a better person and becoming the best me I can be, it's this: I'm far from it.

Like I am screwed up. Terribly damaged and inherently flawed.

There's a passage in the Bible that says,

"I do not understand what I do. For what I want to do I do not do, but what I hate I do . . . For I have the desire to do what is good, but I cannot carry it out. For I do not do the good I want to do, but the evil I do not want to do—this I keep on doing."—Romans 7:15–19

I don't know about you, but I can definitely relate to whoever said this.

As much as I try to be better and do better, I always find myself off the mark.

I don't always do everything perfectly.

I don't do everything right.

And I don't do everything for the right reasons.

Even in my greatest attempt to help others and save the world, I often find myself with a God-complex, thinking that it's actually my job to do so and only I have the power to do it. I often make people projects, dehumanizing them and making their growth and improvement more about scratching my ego. The more passionate I become, the more powerful I become, the easier it somehow is to ignore the pain and to ignore my principles.

As the old saying goes, "Power corrupts and absolute power corrupts absolutely."

I am always at risk of doing the wrong thing with the wrong intentions. Right now as I write this book, I have a complicated mix of good and bad intentions. I want to help people, but there's a part of me that just wants to be different, to be special. To be more than just your average person.

Now some of you may defend me, saying it's normal to want to be different. Hey, thanks, I really appreciate that.

And to your point, I agree. It is normal, to a degree, to not want to simply be another cog in the wheel or a number in the system. However, at least for myself, I know I can greatly underestimate the brokenness of my intentions.

Part of the process in becoming our best selves involves recognizing who we truly are and continually reflecting upon it and reminding ourselves of it. Part of that recognition, as much as we want to ignore it, is recognizing who we are not.

We are not perfect.

We are not always good.

We are not always and completely pure in our motives and intentions.

This is not to imply that we are the absolute worst. That we can do nothing good and nothing with good intentions. We just can't do anything, in my opinion, with pure intentions. If helping or loving another person makes us feel good and better about ourselves, it is hard to define how much we are doing it for another and how much we are doing it for ourselves. (You should watch the *Friends* episode where Phoebe tries to prove to Joey that some actions are completely selfless).

The reality is that you and I are broken.

In the classic Biblical story of the origin of brokenness, God makes a perfect world where the first humans could freely live. God, however, gives them only one rule: do not eat from the Tree of the Knowledge of Good and Evil, or else they will die. As you may know, Adam and Eve eat the fruit from this tree anyway.

Why did they eat the fruit from this tree? Bible teachers suggest they ultimately lacked a strong belief. Adam and Eve did not believe God was good or could be trusted, despite being created by him and having been given only *one* rule. Furthermore, a snake comes along shortly and tells them that the reason God told them not to eat the fruit wasn't because they would die, but because they would know all that God knows. And so, because of their disbelief in God, their desire to be like God, and their desire to define what is good, true and beautiful, they acted upon it.

It starts with a doubt. It evolves into a disbelief. And if left unattended, it turns into a decision.

Murder comes from the disbelief that all human life is valuable and the desire to be the authority that determines the value of each life. Doesn't every crime and tragedy ultimately come from a horrid disbelief in something we all believe and a person's desire to take life and the future into their own hands?

However just because we aren't murderers, thieves, or criminals by law doesn't mean that we too aren't guilty of something.

It may be taking that job or getting into that relationship despite "knowing" you should not, and doing it anyways because you wanted to take life into your hands and define your own path.

Recognize to Resist

Part of becoming and living out your true, best, and beautiful self will require recognizing the ways in which you disbelieve in the greater truths of the world and when you are attempting to take control. It requires recognizing your pain and your ever-present proclivity to ignore it or self-treat it.

In my experience, the most helpful resources for myself in recognizing my own brokenness and propensity for self-treatment is the Enneagram.

BEING IS GREATER THAN DOING

I already mentioned the Enneagram and how it provides a framework towards health and wholeness. It puts to words what fulfills us and what we want to seek in life.

It also creates a framework and puts to words our brokenness.

Each number (personality type) of the Enneagram is associated with a particular fear, desire, and temptation.

1) The Perfectionist: Fear of being bad and a desire to be good. Their temptation is to be judgmental and hypocritical. They are motivated by anger, whether it be resentment towards the world or their parents, or a righteous anger toward the brokenness of the world. Because they are motivated by anger, they are regularly prone to hoarding anger within and eventually releasing it unhealthily onto someone or something.

2) The Helper: Fear of not being loved and a desire to be loved. Their temptation is to not acknowledge their own needs no matter how normal, natural, or good they are. What is interesting is that they are motivated by pride. They believe they deserve the love they desire and will, therefore, do whatever is necessary, in particular manipulating others, to satisfy their need to be loved.

3) The Performer: Fear of being worthless and a desire to be of true value. Their temptation is to put their value into their work, image, and success, thereby motivating them to continually work and improve. The motivation and vice of the Performer is deceit, not so much to others, but rather to themselves. Self-awareness is generally difficult for the Performer. They tell themselves whatever they need to believe in order to achieve what they seek.

4) The Individualist: Fear of being average or having no significance and a desire to be their true self. Their vice is envy. The grass is not only always greener on the other side, but their grass is always brown

whether they can see the other side or not. Because they naturally feel and see this greener grass, their temptation is to fantasize and overindulge in their imagination.

5) The Investigator: Fear of incompetence and a desire to be masters in some body of knowledge. They are major thinkers, but because of this, their temptation is to conceptualize everything; therefore, they don't do anything.

6) The Loyalist: Fear of instability and a desire to have support and stability. The vice of the Loyalist is fear. They are motivated by the fear of the future and, therefore, are continually tempted to be indecisive and seek stability/support.

7) The Enthusiast: Fear of sadness and a desire to be happy. They are motivated by the hunger for happy experiences and possess the vice of gluttony. There is no such thing as too much happiness. Their temptation is to continually think and seek happiness outside of themselves and what they have.

8) The Challenger: Fear of being controlled and powerless and a desire to be in power and protected. Because of this, they are tempted to believe they are self-sufficient and require no one. Their motivation/vice is lust. Though generally associated with sexual desires, lust in its broadest form is the objectification and using of others. The Challenger, in their desire for power, will dominate and force themselves upon others.

9) The Peacemaker: Fear of disruption and separation and a desire, as their name suggests, for peace. The type of peace the Peacemaker desires is not world peace, but rather an internal peace. Because of this desire, their vice is sloth or laziness. Because any good thing or change takes work, the Peacemaker often will be tempted to avoid it and will prefer to choose the life or situation they are comfortable with.

Each of us have learned to cope with this world in one of these nine ways, and it will be necessary for us to recognize how we try to address our fears and fulfill our desires.

Rely

That brings us to the next step in dealing with our brokenness: it requires relying on others. You must rely on the opinion and view of others. As much as you would like to think it, you do not have 360 degree vision, and you are always prone to your own preferred way of looking at your life and world.

Rule and Restructure

Once you have begun the recognition and relying process, you can begin to make the necessary steps to restructure and rule your life. For certain areas of brokenness, you may be capable enough to simply restructure your life to avoid, and eventually relinquish, the grasp certain things or people may have on you.

As we all know, getting into shape is ridiculously difficult. It requires constantly adhering to a set of rules, which need to be constantly adjusted. Our lives, however, are infinitely more difficult and require a much greater adherence to a set of rules as well as continuing adjustment.

All this is to say, no matter how much time you spend crafting a detailed, minute-by-minute schedule, you will always need to review them and restructure.

Remember and Remind

Because our brokenness is so insidious, so dark and secretive, we are always under attack. Always within broadcast of the lie that we are not . . .

Good enough.
Smart enough.
Beautiful enough.
Loveable enough.
Capable enough.
_____ enough.

How many times do you hear these lies and this script in your head throughout your day? It's hard to say. Probably more often than you would like to think or admit. Can you always catch every single one? Probably not. Can you catch some? I think so.

And when you do, when you catch yourself listening to the lies of your childhood and society, you have to resist them and know that you will not die if you do not believe them. When I catch myself in bad thought, in a script of lies, I ask myself, "Is that really true? Is that what I truly believe?"

Remembering and reminding yourself of what is true, good, and beautiful is both necessary for your growth and necessary for your healing and self-preservation. You must continually remind yourself of the truths of your values, wherever you find them and get them from. Whatever your truth is, whatever your mantra, repeat it to yourself, all the time and all day.

Retreat

In times of helplessness, when faced with an addiction too strong to simply resist and restructure, we may need to take more drastic measures. This may require completely removing oneself from that thing, going cold turkey, in order to have a taste of freedom or a moment of clarity. This could take as little as a week to as long as many months if not years.

Most research on the formation of good habits (and I would add the breaking of bad habits) suggests it takes at least four weeks. Depending on the control a bad habit has over you, it could take longer. However, an addict always has an addiction. A recovering alcoholic will always be in recovery. As a recovering narcissist, I will always be in recovery and in constant resistance to my natural desire to make everything about me.

For myself, I often remove myself completely from social media and forms of technology. I have a fairly addictive personality and a narcissistic one at that. Social media is crack for me as it allows me, at any time I want, to search for attention. It's a bitter cycle though because often the more I seek for attention online, the less I get; and the more unfulfilled I find myself, the more I dive deeper and spend longer on my phone. It's a never ending and unhealthy spiral.

And at certain times of extreme risk, of extreme caution to our physical, mental, spiritual and emotional well-being, we must enter ourselves into an intensified type of removal in ways similar to that of rehab. Although rehab is generally associated with drugs and alcohol, I believe we can expand our understanding of addiction to more than simply drugs and alcohol—as we have explored the complexities, dimensions, and depths of holistic health and well-being, we have seen this to be true.

Deepak Chopra has a retreat for those who live with experiences of depression and anxiety. With more and more people courageously acknowledging their illness, this form of rehabilitation or retreat from modern society seems to be very good and very necessary.

I wonder, however, if there are opportunities for more "retreats." Opportunities for us to extract ourselves from all forms of technology and communication. To unplug, disconnect, and learn to be comfortable with oneself and with the silence.

Or what would it look like to have retreats for people who struggle with being single, a place where they can gather in healthy friendship and solitude, learning how to love themselves, and learning to live interdependently with others in healthy and platonic relationships?

Retreats, spiritual or not, can be a healthy and beneficial solution to many if not all city-dwellers as we struggle to find our identity and purpose amidst a busy and over-cluttered world.

There is no shame in not being perfect and not being able to fully determine your life. Sometimes negative things require us to run away from them. And that is okay. I'm not encouraging people to run away from fears or anything uncomfortable, I'm talking about running away from things that should not be in your life.

Replace

No matter how much you may abstain from a particular substance or habit, if it is not replaced by something healthier and better, you will always be at risk of falling back into the old and bad ways.

Don't just resist the brokenness, but replace it with truth, goodness and beauty.

Summary

- We are broken.

- We have broken beliefs and broken behaviors.

- We don't always believe what is true and we don't' always do what is right.

- To be our best we have to recognize our fears, desires, and temptations to disbelieve the truth and take life into our own hands.

- We need to rely on other people to put a mirror to our ugly selves.

- We need to restructure our lives to avoid unnecessary habits.

- We need to resist the lies that we hear and tell ourselves and consciously remind ourselves of what we truly believe.

- Sometimes we need to completely remove ourselves from unhealthy situations.

CONCLUSION

Best Ends with "Est" (French for "Is")

> "It is our choices, Harry, that show what
> we truly are, far more than our abilities."
>
> —J. K. Rowling

> "Your visions will become clear only when you can look into your
> own heart. Who looks outside, dreams; who looks inside, awakes."
>
> —Carl Jung

Writing this book has been one of the most challenging and rewarding journeys of my life. It has challenged me to live up to what I have written but it has also comforted me in reminding me that life truly is a journey.

That I am a work in progress.

That you and I are masterpieces, works of beauty. Yet at the very same time, broken jars of clay.

I have become more convinced than ever that the greatest thing we can do for ourselves and the world is to seek truth, to seek goodness, and to seek beauty. To never stop questioning the lies we've been told, to fight the fears, and to push through the pain. To realize the power and responsibility we have been given. And to live by the truth.

Life can be wonderful.

Life *is* wonderful.

Your life is wonderful.

Discovering who you are and what you are to do in this world is no easy task.

Not in the least.

It requires patience, intention, pro-activity, self-awareness, critical thinking, grace, and a humble heart (along with a list of many other virtues). It involves more than a book or two, a mentor, or a drug trip in South America. There is no quick-fix no easy solution despite every fiber of your body saying there must be. It's a long and hard road.

But the journey, never mind the goal, is so worth it.

It has to be.

In response to Aristotle, the unexamined life is not worth living, but the examined life alone isn't either. Only if and when we both examine our life and explore change will we find ultimate satisfaction. Only then would we ever obtain the good life.

It is my hope, my wish, my prayer that something amidst all of this has helped you.

BEING IS GREATER THAN DOING

Has blessed you.

I hope that through this exploration and journey, you have come a step closer in seeing the truth, goodness, and beauty of life itself, but more importantly, of you and your life.

There is something amazingly true, good, and beautiful about yourself.

It would be a terrible shame to the world if you did not explore it, nourish it and share it.

LAST WORDS

THANK YOU FOR READING!!!

If you've made it to here, I can't help but thank you enough.

PLEASE HELP ME MAKE A DIFFERENCE!!!

If you have enjoyed and more hopefully been blessed by anything that you've read, I would LOVE IT if you would spare literally 1 minute to leave a review of my book on amazon.com.

This helps Amazon know that you liked the book
and that they should recommend it to other people.

EVERY review will also help potential future readers
have more trust in *Being is Great than Doing* when deciding which
book to purchase among the numerous good books out there.

Your review helps more people become their true and better self.
And who doesn't want more authentic and better people out there?

EVERY review makes a difference.
YOUR review makes a difference!

P.S. Let's stay connected!

If you'd like to get the latest thoughts from me,

If you'd like the latest news on my next book,
Whole is Greater than Happy: The Proven Path To True Joy,
subscribe to ryanlui.com

If you think I could be of value to you, your community or
organization, I'd love to connect about speaking at your next event,
contact me at hello@ryanlui.com.

With much love, hope, and appreciation for who you are,
what you are doing and will be doing in this world,

Ryan Lui

97023974R00111

Made in the USA
San Bernardino, CA
21 November 2018